RSPB
CHILDREN'S GUIDE TO

Wildlife

David Chandler, Mike Unwin
& Mark Boyd

A & C BLACK
AN IMPRINT OF BLOOMSBURY
LONDON   NEW DELHI   NEW YORK   SYDNEY

Published 2013 by A&C Black
An imprint of Bloomsbury Publishing Plc
50 Bedford Square, London, WC1B 3DP

www.bloomsbury.com

ISBN 978-1-4081-9246-7

Illustrations: Alan Harris, Peter Hayman, Dave Nurney, Jim
Robins, Laurel Tucker, Dan Zetterstrom, Robin Bouttell, Ian
Jackson, Sandra Pond, Peter Scott,
Chris Shields.

All photographs © Shutterstock.com except:
the photos below supplied by www.rspb-images.com: Nigel Blake: 25
(Nuthatch), 29 (left). Peter Cairns: 13 (Finch).David Broadbent: 14–15,
27 (Puffins). Richard Brooks: 8 (Finch & Redwing), 43 (left). Geoff Dore:
19. Gerald Downey: 25 (Wren), 28 (Curlew). Bob Glover: 8 (& 40–41),
12–13, 16, 23 (Plovers), 23 (& 55), 26 (top & middle), 32 (left), 37, 44
(Rookery), 54–55. Chris Gomersall: 1 (& 22), 6–7 (& 126), 23 (middle),
28 (Shelduck), 30–31 (& 41), 38, 47 (Shearwater), 51 (middle). Jan
Halady: 26 (& 54). Mark Hamblin: 3 (Gannet), 22 (Blue Tit), 25 (Owl),
29 (Eagle), 50 (middle, & 52–53). Tony Hamblin: 5, 29 (Ring Ouzel). Andy
Hay: 10, 27 (mid), 28 (top & bottom), 37 (top), 50 (top), 52. Robert
Horne: 48 (top & bottom). Malcolm Hunt: 45 (Martin). Ernie Janes: 47
(feeder). Ray Kennedy: 5 (Curlew) & 22 (Blackbird). David Kjaer: 3 (top)
& 45, 24 (middle). Steve Knell: 22–23 (& 46), 33 (top). Chris Knights:
2–3 (& 44–45), 23 (Finches), 29 (Grouse). Mike Lane: 6 (L-t Tit), 13
(Coal Tit) & 22 (Sparrow), 24 (Dunnock), 29 (top), 37 (Tit), 44 (top &

bottom), 45 (Puffin). Gordon Langsbury: 5 (Wagtail), 8 (Blackcap), 42
(Blackbird), 48 (Geese), 50 (Hoopoe), 55. George McCarthy: 9. Carolyn
Merrett 4, 5, 11, 14, 35, 39, 53. Bill Paton: 6 (Tit). Mike Read: 29 (S'chat),
34–35, 35 (bottom), 43 (Owl), 47 (top). Richard Revels: 32 (right), 46
(top). Geoff Simp-son: 46 (middle). Roger Tidman: 27 (top), 51 (bottom).
David Tipling: 22 (Robin), 24 (top), 36 (bottom). David White: 36 (top).
Roger Wilmshurst: 42 (top), 48 (pier).

Other photos supplied by:
Dawn Balmer/BTO 53. Tim Bonnett/RSPB Optics: 15. Pete Cairns/
Windrush: 49. David Chandler: 15 (bottom); 21 & 30 (all). David
Tipling: 17 (both). Claire Tochel 47. p149 © Padmayogini/Shutterstock.
com; p167 © hazelisles via Wikimedia Commons. Copyright in the
photographs remains with the individuals and organisations credited
above.

A CIP catalogue for this book is available from the British
Library.

MIX
Paper from
responsible sources
FSC® C008047

Printed in China by C&C Offset Printer Co., Ltd

10 9 8 7 6 5 4 3 2 1

Contents

Contents

Wildlife Activities

What is birding?

Different people enjoy birds in different ways. Some travel the world to see as many species as possible. Others watch their local birds, or just those that visit their garden. Some watch birds on their own, some with friends and some in bigger groups. You can watch birds, study birds, draw birds, photograph birds, write about birds and put rings on birds!
Some people call it bird watching, others call it birding, but the fact is there are many, many ways to enjoy birds.

Curlew

You're not alone

If you're reading this, you probably already like birds. You may not know many other people who do, but there are plenty, including young people. You are likely to meet other bird fans as you go along – it's a great way of making new friends!

Using the book

This section is divided into two parts to help you get the most out of your birding. The first part will help you with some of the skills you need to enjoy birds to the full. The second part is a guide to the birds you are most likely to see first – the common and more obvious species. Put them together and you have the perfect short cut to being a better birder.

Grey wagtail

HOOKED!

A little interest in birding can easily become a lifelong passion. Watching birds can be exciting, challenging, relaxing and rewarding. It can change the way you see places you know, and can take you to new places. You may become hooked on other wildlife too, like butterflies, dragonflies or bats, so watch out!

You can watch birds however you like, wherever you like – it's up to you. But most of all, have fun, because the best birder is the one who enjoys it the most.

Identification

Most people want to know the name of the bird they are looking at. Some birds are easy to identify; some are not. When you start birding, trying to put the right name to a bird can be difficult and confusing. You will probably get some wrong, but don't give up. It gets easier and, with practice, you will get more of them right. Collect as many clues about the bird as you can.

Size

Bird books give birds' lengths in centimetres. Imagine the bird lying flat on its back. Its length is measured from the tip of the bill, over the top of the head and down the back, all the way to the tip of the tail. But that's not how you see birds in the wild.

The lengths in books help you to work out whether one species is bigger than another – but remember that they include the bill and tail. Long-tailed tits are tiny birds, but because of their long tail, their length in a book suggests that they are as big as great tits.

Great tits (above) and long-tailed tits (left) are not the same size, even though the books say they are!

You can't see centimetres when you look at a living, wild bird. So, instead, compare the bird's size to a species you know – if possible, one you can see at the same time (e.g. "about the size of a blackbird"; "pigeon-sized"; "smaller than a starling").

TOP TIPS

Take care if the sun is behind the bird. The edges of the bird will be less visible and the bird will look smaller and darker than it really is.

Watch out, especially in cold weather, for birds with fluffed-up feathers – they will look bigger than they are normally.

Compare the shape of your mystery bird with a bird you know. Is it like a sparrow? A pigeon? A duck? This will help you get to the right part of the field guide and makes identification easier.

Some bird shapes: Swallow, wader, pigeon, thrush, duck, gull, sparrow.

Make a note of obvious features or striking colours. Then, try to

Colour and markings

describe the whole bird from head to tail, including upperparts, underparts, bill and legs. Use the labels on pages 12–13 to help you. Be patient – you might not see everything without waiting and watching. These words will help too:

wing-bar: an obvious mark across a closed wing, or along an open wing. When a ringed plover flies, you can see its white wing-bar.

moustache or moustachial stripes: stripes starting near the beak and going down the bird's 'face'. Male reed buntings in summer plumage have a white moustache.

bars or barring: lines going across a bird's plumage. A sparrowhawk has barring on its underparts.

streaks or streaking: lines along (not across) a bird's plumage. A meadow pipit has streaks on its breast and flanks.

window: a pale area, usually found on the front edge of a bird's primaries. Normally used in descriptions of gulls. Herring gulls have white windows.

fingers: the spread feathers of a bird's wing-tips in flight, which look like fingers. You can often see fingers on buzzards.

speculum: a bright patch of colour on a duck's wing. The male mallard has a shiny blue speculum.

Colour confusion

Colours don't always look the same, or the same as the picture in the field guide. The direction and brightness of the sun can change a bird's appearance. If a bird has been feeding in the mud, it might be hard to see its colours – especially on its legs and beak. Old feathers, which have been out in the wind, rain and sun for up to a year, might look paler than fresh, unworn feathers and their coloured tips may have worn off.

Some good field marks:
woodpigeon – white
wing flash;
male bullfinch – red breast and black cap; male blackcap –
black cap; redwing – rusty flanks and creamy eyebrows.

Behaviour

Look at what the bird is doing and how it is moving. Does it hop, walk or run? Does it fly along in a straight line or fly up and down in a wiggly line? Does it flap all the time, or glide? What a bird does can give you important clues. In the UK, a bird hovering by a motorway is almost certainly a kestrel (though buzzards sometimes hover for short periods of time). Nuthatches climb up and down tree trunks – Treecreepers only climb up them.

The sounds birds make can tell you a lot. Chiffchaffs and willow warblers look almost the same, but their songs are completely different. You might think bird songs are too hard to learn. But make the effort to learn some of the easier ones – it will change and improve your birding. Once you know most common bird calls, an unusual one will stand out.

Recordings can be helpful and there are lots to chose from (see page 55). There is even special software for loading onto an MP3 player. But the best way to learn bird song is to hear it for real, find the bird that's making the noise and identify it. Birding with someone who already knows some bird songs can be useful, too.

Treecreeper. Climbs up the trunk only.

TOP TIP

Cup your hands behind your ears and listen. Noises coming from in front of you will sound louder.

Try using words to describe songs you hear – or try drawing them (see diagram above). Remember that not all the noises birds make come from their beaks. Woodpigeons and nightjars clap their wings together; great and lesser spotted woodpeckers drum with their beaks on trees; and breeding snipe make a wonderful bleating noise by diving through the air with some tail feathers sticking out!

Time and place

If your field guide has maps, use them to find out where the bird lives. There are no lesser spotted woodpeckers in the north of Scotland. If you see a black-and-white woodpecker there it has to be a great spotted. Take care though. Maps can be small and it's hard to see exactly where a bird's range finishes. Some may be out of date, too – bird ranges change, though not normally very quickly.

Not all the birds you see are with us all the time. Some are here just in summer, some just in winter. Some are 'passage visitors' – they stop here on their way to somewhere else. They are 'on passage' and don't breed or spend the winter here.

Natural habitat

Migrating birds can turn up anywhere, but you'll normally find birds in their natural habitat. Use habitat information to help you identify birds. Cormorants and shags look similar. But if you see a cormorant-shaped bird inland, a long way from the sea, it's not likely to be a shag.

Cormorants used to be found only on the coast. Now they're often seen inland.

TOP TIPS

If you are birding somewhere new, before you go find out which birds you are likely to see and what they look like.

If you are trying to decide whether you've seen a common bird or a rare one that looks very similar, it's probably the common one.

The most reliable identifications are based on more than one feature. Look for as many features as possible.

Taking notes

When you find a bird that you can't identify, notes (or photos, see 'Start digiscoping', page 53) will help you remember what you see. Making a simple sketch and using a few words to describe the bird is a good way to do this. You don't need to be a good artist. Even if the sketch doesn't look like the bird, it will help you remember what you saw.

Note down as much information as possible. Don't forget to record the date, place, time and weather. But concentrate on the bird first – you can do these other bits after the bird has gone. Sketching and describing a bird is a skill. You will get better at it. It makes you look hard at the bird, which helps to build up your skills.

Learn to turn eggs into birds. This is a great way to create simple bird shapes for sketches.

These egg shapes help make up simple outlines of a duck, a sparrow and a heron.

Using your bird book

Use your field guide when you are out birding – don't keep it at home. A good guide can help you work out what you should look for, to be sure of your identification. But take care not to 'see' things that aren't really there, just so you match the description in the book. And try not to spend all your time looking in the book – the bird might fly off!

Getting going

Putting names to birds is enjoyable and challenging. When you start, it's not easy. If you don't see a bird well, identification will be difficult. Don't give up. The more you practise, the better you will get. Going birding with someone more experienced can help, but don't just let them tell you the birds' names. Ask them how they know. Try to work out the birds for yourself; your skills will improve faster. Identification is just the beginning. When you know what the bird is, then you can begin to find out more about it.

Sketching wild birds will help you get to know them much better.

Feathers

Birds are the only animals with feathers. Feathers help birds to fly, control their temperature, attract a mate and hide from predators. Knowing more about feathers will also help you to identify birds.

How feathers grow

It may be hard to tell, but feathers grow from distinct areas on a bird's body – they don't grow evenly over the whole body surface. Feathers overlap one another, a bit like roof tiles. This streamlines a bird for flight and helps to keep the wind and rain out. All of the feathers put together make up a bird's plumage.

Feathers grow out of the bird's skin and, like hair or fur, are dead when fully grown. They get worn and damaged easily and are replaced at least once a year. New feathers grow and push out the old ones. This is called moult. Most birds replace all of their feathers once a year after they have bred. Some replace some of their feathers before the breeding season, too.

When you look at a bird, apart from its bill and legs, most of what you see is feathers. Knowing the names of the different feather groups makes describing a bird easier. The pictures on these two pages show the most important feather groups, as well as other parts of a bird's body. See page 7 for more bird words.

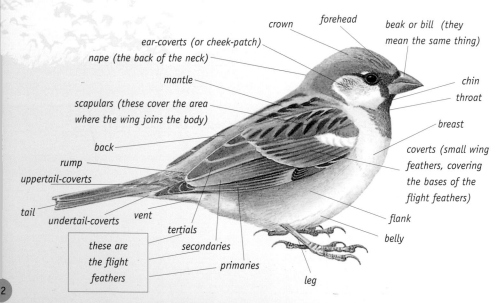

crown

forehead

beak or bill (they mean the same thing)

ear-coverts (or cheek-patch)

nape (the back of the neck)

mantle

chin

throat

scapulars (these cover the area where the wing joins the body)

breast

back

coverts (small wing feathers, covering the bases of the flight feathers)

rump

uppertail-coverts

tail

undertail-coverts

vent

flank

belly

tertials

secondaries

these are the flight feathers

primaries

leg

primaries – the long flight feathers attached to the 'hand' of the wing

secondaries – the shorter flight feathers attached to the 'arm' of the wing. The ones nearest the bird's body are called tertials.

lesser coverts – the smallest coverts

median coverts – middle-sized coverts

greater coverts – the biggest coverts

alula – very small feathers that are raised up to smooth the air flow and stop a bird falling out of the air when it is landing

primary coverts – the coverts over the bases of the primaries

eyebrow or supercilium (a stripe over the eye)

lores (the area between the base of the bill and the eye)

eye-stripe (a stripe through the eye)

moustache/moustachial stripe

Below left: A lot of the yellow in a greenfinch wing is on the edges of the primaries.
Below right: White tips on a coal tit's coverts make two wing-bars.

The kit

You can enjoy birds without any equipment, but there are a few things you will need if you really want to get involved. The basic kit is binoculars, a field guide and a notebook.

Binoculars

For finding birds and seeing them better

Not all binoculars (or 'bins') are good for watching birds. Read this before you buy. If someone else is buying binoculars for you, get them to read this first.

Good birding binoculars:

- are not too heavy. You might be wearing them all day. Heavy bins are difficult to hold steady too

- feel comfortable in your hands

- have eyepieces that fold close enough together for you to see one circle when you look through them, without black shapes appearing

- are clear and bright when you look through them

- focus easily – focusing should be smooth and not too stiff. Try them on something close and something far away. If you want to look at butterflies or dragonflies, make sure they focus down to about two metres or less

- don't need to cost too much

What the numbers mean

Two numbers are used to describe binoculars. For example 8x32, or 10x42. The first number is the magnification – how many times bigger the bird will look. 8x32 binoculars magnify eight times. The second number is the diameter (width) of the big lenses at the front (the objective lenses). 10x42s have 42mm objectives. Bigger objectives let in more light and give a brighter image. Binoculars that magnify seven or eight times, and have objectives that are 30–42mm wide are very good for birding. Magnifications up to ten times are OK, but are harder to hold steady.

Compacts

If you find full-size binoculars too big to hold, try compacts. These are smaller and lighter than standard bins. They have objective lenses of less than 30mm. They may not be as bright to look through, but many give a view that is fine for birding. If you have small hands, compacts may be a good way to get started. Choose a magnification of seven or eight times.

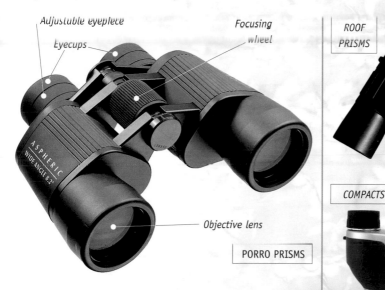

Adjustable eyepiece

Eyecups

Focusing wheel

ROOF PRISMS

COMPACTS

Objective lens

PORRO PRISMS

Binoculars come in different shapes and sizes. Any of these designs could be a good choice for you, but try them first.

Waterproof?

Not all binoculars are waterproof. Try to get a rainguard. This will keep the worst of the weather off the eyepieces. It protects the lenses from crumbs when you eat your lunch too! If it rains hard, tuck your binoculars inside your coat to keep them dry.

Smart shopping

If you can, buy from a specialist binocular shop with staff that know about birding. The UK bird watching links website (see pages 52 and 55) will give you some ideas of where to shop, or you can look at adverts in

Above: Using a rainguard.

birding magazines (see page 52). Decide how much you can spend, and look at a small number of binoculars that you can afford. You can get good binoculars without spending too much money, especially if you buy second-hand. Get the best you can afford. The easier they are to use, and the better the image you see through them, the more you will enjoy birding.

Strapping up

Put the strap on your binoculars and hang them around your neck. Always use the strap – it will stop you dropping your binoculars. Make sure the strap isn't too long – they should hang just below your chest. You can buy elasticated straps that are slightly 'bouncy'. These are more comfortable and make binoculars feel lighter.

Setting your sights

Your right eye may be different to your left eye, so your binoculars need to be set up to suit them both. One eyepiece will be adjustable – normally the right one. Different binoculars are adjusted in different ways. Keep both eyes open when you make adjustments.

1. Cover the right-hand objective with one hand. Use the central focusing to focus the left side on something with a clear outline 50–100m away – a chimney pot or TV aerial maybe.

Above and left: Binoculars give a great view of this jay.

2. When the left-hand side is focused, cover up this side and use the eyepiece adjustment to focus the right side. When that side is clear, make a note of the number on the dial and keep this eyepiece set there whenever you use the binoculars.
3. Now all you need to do is use the central focusing for any bird you are looking at – however near or far away it is.

Glasses

If you wear glasses you may need to wear them when you are using binoculars (not everyone has to). To use binoculars with glasses you need to adjust the eye-cups. If the eye-cups are rubber, fold them down. If they are plastic, twist or push them down. Try it out when you buy the binoculars to make sure it works for you.

Practice makes perfect

When you are birding keep your binoculars around your neck, not inside their case. You might find it hard to find birds with your binoculars that you can see with

your naked eyes. Keep your eyes on the bird and bring your binoculars up to your eyes. If you find it difficult, practise when you're not birding – on different things around your garden maybe.

Learn which way to turn the focusing wheel to focus on more distant birds or closer ones – you don't want to waste time doing this when you're trying to look at an exciting bird! Practise focusing quickly – you could do this in the garden, too.

Above: Adjust the eyepiece to get the clearest view.

Handle with care

Protect your binoculars from bumps. Keep the lenses clean but don't clean them too often. Every time you clean them you risk scratching them. When you clean them, blow on the lenses first to get rid of crumbs, dust and sand. Lens tissues or lens cloths are the best things to clean the lenses with.

Below: Don't use your binoculars just to look for birds you've already seen. Search for birds with them too.

For identifying birds and learning more about them

A field guide is a book that has been designed for use indoors or out ('in the field'). A good field guide will help you put the right names to the birds you see and tell you something about them. The words and pictures will tell you what different birds look like, where and when you might see them and how common they are. They even tell you what sounds birds make, though these can be hard to describe (see page 9). Your field guide will help you to tell males from females, young birds from adults and birds in breeding plumage from birds in non-breeding plumage.

Good guides

There are many different field guides. Some are very good, others are not. Field guides that contain only photos are not normally as useful as those with illustrations. It's hard to get photos that show all the different features of each bird. To get you started, this book includes a field guide to the birds you are most likely to see when you start birding (see pages 56–125). Sooner or later though, you will need a guide that describes more birds than we could fit in this book. We recommend three good ones:

Recommendation 1 – for more detail

RSPB Handbook of British Birds covers the 280 most common birds in the UK – so you won't get confused by other European species. It includes lots of information about how birds live – much more than most field guides.

Recommendation 2 – for more birds

Pocket Guide to the Birds of Britain and North-West Europe covers 380 species, including most European species. It's the most compact of the three recommended guides and helps if you go on holiday to other parts of Europe.

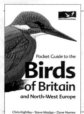

Recommendation 3 – for even more birds

Collins Bird Guide covers over 700 species – all of the birds of the UK and Europe. Many people think this is the best field guide. It is very good, but all those species might confuse you when you are first learning your birds.

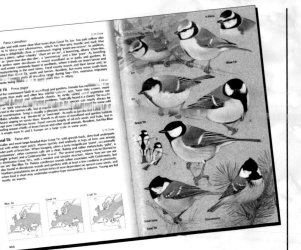

In really good field guides, such as the three guides on the left and Birds of Europe by Lars Jonsson (above), the words, pictures and maps for a species can all be seen at the same time. This makes the book easier to use. Field guide maps tell you where each species can be seen at different times of the year.

Left and below: Real birds vary, and don't always look exactly like their paintings in a book. And paintings can vary from one book to another. Compare these two field guide illustrations of Fulmars with the real birds in the photo above.

Remember also that a photo can make a bird look darker or paler, depending on the light. Try to use a combination of pictures and other clues to help get your identification right.

Get book-wise!

Make the most of your field guide:

● Read the introduction. It will explain the key features of your guide, and how to use them.

● Look through your field guide as often as you can at home. Get to know the names of the birds and what they look like.

● Learn where in the book to find different birds. Most bird books have the birds in more or less the same order. This is the order used by scientists. We have used it in this book's field guide.

● Don't worry about the book getting creased or dirty. It's a tool to be used. Use it at home and when you are out birding. Scribble notes in it, if you like.

● Most birders have more than one field guide, so that they can compare different descriptions and pictures of the same bird.

● You can install field guide software on a PDA or MP3 player. They're easy to carry when you're out bird watching, and you can hear what birds sound like, too. There are also DVD-ROMs to use at home.

A birding notebook

So you don't forget!

You don't have to use a notebook – not all birders do. But notebooks are a good way of recording what you see and making notes about birds you can't identify. If you don't record things on the spot you will quickly forget. Your notes don't have to be just for the 'science' of birding. You can jot down how birds make you feel, or even what you had for lunch! Notebooks are good for reading later, too. You can look back and remember great days out birding, months or even years later. It can also help you build up a picture of your birding and let you see how the birds in the places you go change throughout the year.

Some notes and a quick sketch of a mystery duck. Use the field guide (pages 56–125) to help you identify it. The answer is below in case you get stuck.

Take note

A good birding notebook:

- fits in your pocket

- is tough enough to stay in one piece even after lots of birding trips

- has a cover hard enough for leaning on

- opens flat enough to be easy to write in.

Answer: The mystery duck is a Pochard.

You can use a pencil or a pen to take notes. Some notebooks have special pen holders. Others have spiral binding you could keep your pen in. Elastic bands make good bookmarks and stop the pages flapping around.

When you have finished a notebook, remember not to throw it out – even if you think it's rubbish. Birders like looking back over their old notebooks. Their first ones are particularly special.

Write and draw things in your notebook when you are out bird watching.

Be creative

You can do whatever you like in your notebook. If you like writing, make notes about what birds do and what their colours remind you of. Use your notes back home to help you write a story or poem. If you like art, draw or paint wild birds in different positions and doing different things. You could even enter 'AllWrite' or 'WildArt', competitions organised by RSPB Wildlife Explorers.

The information in your notebook could be part of a project that you work on at home. This is the work of Tobias Nowlan, a keen teenage birder.

Alternative records

Instead of a notebook, you could try:

● a checklist (a printed list of bird species). Just tick off the ones you see, or record your counts of different species.

● a mobile phone. Make notes on it, and set the alarm so you remember to look at them later, or e-mail them to yourself! If you have a cameraphone, and a telescope, you can use your phone to take photos of birds too.

● a PDA with special bird-recording software.

Habitats

Different birds live in different places, called habitats. The next eight pages will help you enjoy birds in a range of habitats.

Gardens and parks

Your garden or a local park is a great place to start birding. You can watch birds often and get to know some common species well.

Robin and blackbird. Easy to see and interesting.

● Make your garden attractive to birds. Provide food, water and nesting places (see pages 36–37).

● Learn the differences between blue and great tits, song thrushes and blackbirds, dunnocks and house sparrows, collared doves and woodpigeons.

● Watch bird behaviour. Which birds drive others away? Where do different species feed?

● House sparrows, starlings, swifts, house martins and jackdaws nest in chimneys, roofs and gutters. Robins sometimes nest in sheds!

● In the summer, watch the sky for swifts, swallows and house martins.

● Visit parks when there are not too many people around. Make sure a grown-up knows what you're doing.

● Play areas with swings and slides aren't good for birds. Parks with grassy areas, trees, bushes and water are better.

Other garden and park birds to look for: great spotted woodpecker, song thrush, redwing, fieldfare, blackcap, coal tit, long-tailed tit, siskin, greenfinch, chaffinch, goldfinch, magpie.

Above: blue tit.
Left: robin, blackbird, house sparrow.

Fields and hedges

Most of the UK is farmland. Some farms have animals, like cows, sheep or pigs, others just grow cereals, vegetables or fruit. Many wild birds live on farmland too, with different birds on different types of farms.

Goldfinches. The yellow wing-bars are obvious.

- Watch hedges carefully for tits, finches, buntings thrushes and warblers. Bigger trees, and hedges with more than one type of tree or bush, are the best.

- In winter, check bare fields for flocks of birds such as gulls, woodpigeons and stock Doves, lapwings and golden plovers, rooks and jackdaws, starlings, redwings and fieldfares, finches, buntings, skylarks.

- Lapwing, redshank and snipe breed in damp, grassy areas.

- Look up and listen for skylarks – they sing from February until mid-summer in some places.

- If there's rough grassland, try an early morning or late evening visit – and hope for a barn owl.

Yellowhammer

Take care. Make sure you are allowed to be there and that it's safe. Don't walk across farm fields unless there is a public right of way. Make sure a grown-up knows what you're doing.

Other farmland birds to look for: buzzard, little owl, turtle dove, swallow, whitethroat, bullfinch.

Left: Skylark
Far left: If you see lapwings, look for golden plovers too. There aren't any here though!

Woodland

Wherever you live, there is probably woodland nearby. Even small patches are worth exploring. Woodlands are made up of deciduous trees (most of which have no leaves in the winter), coniferous trees (most of which have leaves all year round) or a mixture of both. Deciduous or mixed

A willow warbler's song will help you tell it from a chiffchaff.

woodlands are normally best for birding. Woodland birds may be there, but they can be hard to see.

● Walk slowly and stop often. Use your eyes and ears. Learn the common woodland species' songs. The chiffchaff's is easy to learn in early spring, but don't confuse it with the great tit's *tea-cher* song.

● Look for bird movement – from tree to tree, between leaves and twigs and on trunks and branches.

● Sit and watch. Sometimes you see more by waiting than by walking. A pool where birds drink is a good place to watch.

● Don't just look up. Look at ground level for thrushes, wrens and dunnocks and higher up for finches, tits, pigeons and warblers. Check trunks and branches for woodpeckers, nuthatches, treecreepers and sometimes, tits.

Above: The sparrowhawk's silent, twisting flight make it a deadly predator.

Right: Dunnocks are handsome and have a sweet singing voice. But not everyone notices them.

● In spring and early summer migrants arrive and many birds sing. Go birding before the leaves come out and block your view! The beginning and end of the day are best.

- The wood's sheltered side (away from the wind) may have more birds in it. Look for sunny patches. Insects are more active there, and insects are good bird food!

- Glades and clearings are lighter, contain different plants and attract insects. They are another good feeding area for birds.

- Watch the edge of the wood from outside – you can see the whole height of the trees, which isn't easy from inside the wood.

- In winter look for mixed tit flocks – blue tits and great tits searching for food together. Sometimes other species join the flock – goldcrests, a treecreeper or other tit species. If you don't find the flock, you might think there are no birds in the wood! You may hear high-pitched squeaks and harsh chattering before you see the flock.

Nuthatch (top) and wren (above). Two woodland birds with loud voices.

- Search coniferous woods for coal tit, goldcrest, mistle thrush, and siskin.

- Enjoy an upland oak wood in the summer, and look for pied flycatcher, redstart and wood warbler.

Other woodland birds to look for: sparrowhawk, buzzard, stock dove, tawny owl, blackcap, garden warbler, willow warbler, spotted flycatcher, marsh tit, willow tit.

Tawny owl. Voles beware!

Lakes

Lakeside bird watching can be wonderful. Birds feed over, on and under the water, and around muddy shores. They rest and nest on islands and vegetation. Trees and bushes nearby provide even more opportunities for birds.

Wigeon breed in Iceland, Scandinavia and Siberia. Thousands winter in the UK.

Stay safe. Take care around steep or slippery banks, or soft mud.

Grey heron. One of our biggest birds.

● Scan the whole lake several times. Birds dive or hide behind islands and in vegetation – you won't see everything in one look.

● Common terns, canada geese and mute swans nest on islands. In winter, look for roosting ducks and gulls, and cormorants wing-drying.

● Check gull and duck flocks carefully. There may be more than one species in there!

● Kingfishers fly low and fast over the water. Look for an orange and blue blur. They perch in trees overhanging the water, or on posts sticking out of the water. Get used to their high-pitched whistle.

● Swifts, swallows, house martins and sand martins feed on insects over water. Hobbies may feed on these insect-eaters.

● Check the vegetation around the edges for reed warblers and sedge warblers (you'll probably hear them first), and also for reed buntings.

Other lake birds to look for: great crested grebe, little grebe, grey heron, wigeon, teal, gadwall, shoveler, tufted duck, pochard, goldeneye, little ringed plover, green sandpiper, grey wagtail.

Kingfisher. Stunning!

Gulls often gather in large flocks. Most of these are black-headed gulls. Can you see any that aren't?

The UK coastline includes sandy beaches, pebbly beaches, rocky cliffs and islands. Some bits are wild; others are packed with holiday-makers. There are always birds to look for.

● Enjoy puffins, guillemots, razorbills, kittiwakes and gannets at a noisy, smelly seabird colony! In Ireland, and Scotland there are black guillemots too.

● If there are cliffs, there could be fulmars, relatives of albatrosses. Peregrines and kestrels nest on cliffs too.

● Look out to sea. There could be cormorants, shags, eiders, gulls, terns and bright white gannets. Don't look just once – birds fly past, dive, or disappear behind waves.

● Gulls come close. Have a good look at them. It takes four years for herring gulls to become adults. Use a field guide to work out how old they are.

● Little terns and ringed plovers nest on shingle beaches. There may be fences to protect them. Take care not to disturb them.

● Rock pipits like rocky areas, and sanderlings like sandy beaches.

● Turnstones, starlings, rock pipits, carrion crows and hooded crows like feeding along high tide lines.

Other coastal birds to look for: eider, purple sandpiper, sandwich tern, stonechat, raven, jackdaw.

Gannets nest close together at a gannetry.

Puffins

Estuaries

Estuaries are where rivers join the sea. When the tide goes out, mud is uncovered. It's stuffed with invertebrates, excellent food for waders and wildfowl, especially in the winter and during migration.

Dunlins in winter plumage. They have lost the black belly of their breeding plumage.

● Check the tide times in local papers, the internet, *The Birdwatchers' Yearbook* or birding magazines. Visit just before high tide for the best views.

● Keep the sun behind you or it may be difficult to see colours clearly.

● Scan more than once. Birds move, dive and hide.

● Learn the most common waders – oystercatcher, ringed plover, lapwing, knot, turnstone, dunlin, redshank and curlew. Then it's easier to spot something unusual.

Shelduck

● When a flock suddenly takes off, look for a hunting Peregrine.

● Look at the water too. There could be grebes, ducks, geese, swans, gulls and cormorants.

● If there are hides, use them! They can give great, close views and are warmer.

Curlew

Be careful: don't walk out on the mud. It can be very soft and the tide can come in quickly. Estuaries can be cold, so dress to stay warm and dry.

Other estuary birds to look for: great crested grebe, grey heron, shelduck, wigeon, pintail, rock pipit.

Grey plovers – big and chunky. And a dunlin.

Hills and mountains

Buzzard

Most of our 'uplands' (hills and mountains) are in the north and west. There aren't many kinds of upland birds, but some of them are hard to see anywhere else.

● Walk a little, stop and scan. Look for movement and birds perched on boulders or fences. Watch the sky.

● This is grouse country. Red grouse are the easiest to see.

● Meadow pipits are common. Their *see-see-see* call and song flights give them away. Don't confuse them with skylarks.

● A small bird with a white rump flying away is probably a wheatear.

Red grouse – with wonderful red 'eyebrows'.

● Look for stonechats and whinchats. Stonechats are easier to see; whinchats prefer damper areas.

● Predators include merlins, hen harriers, peregrines, and, in scotland, golden eagles. Short-eared owls breed on some moors. This owl flies in daylight!

● Watch out for ravens – don't mistake them for birds of prey, carrion crows or hooded crows.

● Some waders breed here. They look fantastic, especially dunlin and golden plover. Look for curlew, snipe, redshank and lapwing, too.

Don't go to the uplands on your own. Take an adult with you – they can be dangerous places and it is easy to get lost.

Other upland birds to look for: black grouse, cuckoo, twite, ring ouzel.

From left to right: whinchat, golden eagle, stonechat and ring ouzel.

Where to go

You don't need to travel far to see birds. Wherever you live, there will be some nearby. Start by spending time getting to know your local birds. The better you know the common species, the easier it will be to identify something unusual. Your garden or a local park is a good starting point.

A local patch

Once you're familiar with your immediate surroundings, find somewhere else nearby with more bird variety. Birders call this a 'local patch'. Watching a local patch is a great thing to do. It's easy, because it's close, and you learn a lot by watching the same area regularly. There may be no other people looking at birds there, so any information you collect could be useful for conservation too (see page 40).

When you are going birding, always make sure that a grown-up knows where you are going and what you will be doing.

A good local patch:

- has a variety of habitats – so there's a bigger variety of birds

- has open water, such as a pond or river – but don't worry if you can't find anywhere with water

- is easy to get to – you can walk or cycle there quickly

- needs no more than an hour and a half for a visit

- is a safe place to go.

REAL LOCAL PATCHES

You can see on the map that Areas A and B are close together. They are different parts of the same local patch. In Area A (top) green woodpeckers and fieldfares feed in the paddocks and yellowhammers use the hedges. Area B (middle) is a scrubby area good for seeing whitethroat, linnet and willow warbler.

Area C (bottom) is a different local patch, with open water and strips of woodland around the edges. Great crested grebes breed here and common sandpipers visit during migration.

Using a map

To find a local patch talk to local people you know, or use an Ordnance Survey (OS) map. You might be surprised at what's nearby, even if you think you know your area well. Maps come in different scales. If you can find one, use a 1:25,000 scale map. This has more detail than a 1:50,000 map. If there are no maps at home, a library may have some. Alternatively visit the OS website – www.ordnancesurvey.co.uk/oswebsite/getamap – you can look at small areas of maps online and print them.

Use the key on the map to find out if there is water or woodland, both of which are good in a local patch. Or choose an area with trees and rough grassland, or an old churchyard. There are no rules; just find somewhere with a bit of variety. The map will help you work out where you are allowed to walk. Look for 'public rights of way' and 'other public access' on the key.

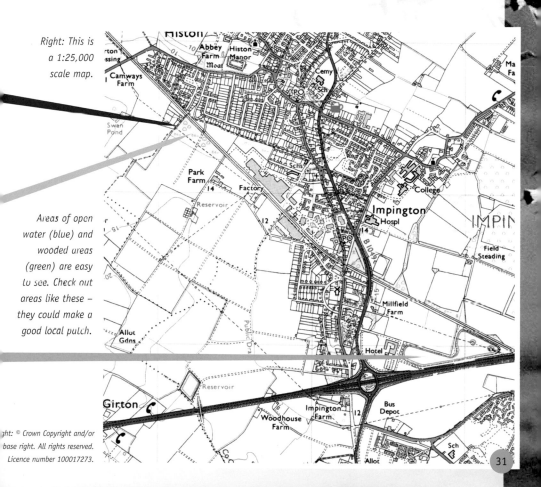

Right: This is a 1:25,000 scale map.

Areas of open water (blue) and wooded areas (green) are easy to see. Check out areas like these – they could make a good local patch.

Keep visiting

Get to know your local patch well. Go there often, at different times of day and different times of year. After a while, you will get to know its birds very well – probably better than anyone else.

Try to work out:

- which birds live where

- whether a bird is there all year round (a resident species) or just for part of the year (a migrant species)

- what the different species sound like

- which species look different from winter to summer, and when their appearance changes

- whether birds are doing different things at different times of year.

Once you're hooked, you will want to go to other good bird places, too.

Further from home

Travelling a short distance could bring even more birds within your reach. But to do this, you need to know where to go, and be able to get there. Here are some ideas to help you find the best birding places to visit:

- ask any local birders you know

- look in your county bird report at your local library or at your local bird club

- look in a site guide ("Where to Watch Birds" books). These cover different parts of the UK and Ireland

Turtle dove

Spotted flycatcher

- look in the *Birdwatcher's Yearbook* (see page 55)

- get on the web. If your local bird club has a website, that might help. Some national birding websites are useful, too (see pages 52 and 55).

You might be able to cycle or use public transport to get to some of the sites safely. This isn't always possible, so you may have to persuade someone to take you, or find out if there is a local RSPB Wildlife Explorers group (see page 54). If there is, they may organise trips to good bird sites.

Lesser spotted woodpecker

Family days out – visiting nature reserves

You may live near a nature reserve. If you don't, finding a way to visit one is a challenge you could set yourself. There are more than you may think, and many are near towns. Visit the RSPB's website to find out more about its nature reserves. Check out the Wildfowl and Wetlands Trust and your local Wildlife Trust websites, too.

Remember: to see a variety of birds, you need to visit a variety of habitats. Pages 22–29 describe birds and bird watching in some different habitats. Don't forget to tell a grown-up where you are going. They might want to come with you – if they do, make sure they see some birds too!

Three ways to find some good bird watching sites.

Birding action

Once you've got your binoculars and found a good place to look for birds, what next? How can you improve your chances? Experienced bird watchers make it look easy. This section tells you how.

Getting closer to birds

You don't need to dress like a commando in full camouflage gear! Dull-coloured clothes are generally better than bright colours, but it's more important that what you wear protects you from the weather. This might mean gloves, a hat (that doesn't cover your ears, or you won't hear birds very well) and lots of layers in winter, or a sunhat and suncream in summer. Wellington boots are good if you're going to wet or muddy places. Try to wear clothes that don't rustle too much – it will be easier to hear birds.

When to go

You can see or hear birds at almost any time of day, but some times are better than others. The worst time is normally the middle of the day, especially during really hot weather. One hour after dawn is the most active time for birds, but late afternoon and early evening are good times too. Waders and other birds that feed when the tide goes out are different. They will feed in the middle of the night if the tide is right!

The right approach

How you move is more important than what you wear. Move slowly and gently, looking carefully for signs of bird movement. Stop and look around frequently. With practice you will see the difference between a twig moving in the wind and a warbler moving in a treetop. Look up and behind you, too. Use your ears – you will hear many birds before you see them. Some you may hear but never see – such as cuckoos or tawny owls.

Move carefully and use cover to get closer to birds.

ToP TIP

Use your binoculars to **search** for birds. Don't use them just to look at birds you have already found with your naked eyes. Habitat edges – where one habitat meets another – are good places to look. Pages 22–29 give you some more ideas.

A good viewpoint

When you can, keep the sun behind you or to one side. It's difficult to see birds well if you're looking into the sun. Keeping trees, bushes, hedges or a slight rise in the land between you and the birds makes it easier to get closer. You can stalk birds by getting down low, or even lying on your belly. This can be an exciting way of getting some good, close views. Try not to stand on the skyline – your shape will be very obvious and nervous birds will fly away.

Hides are for everyone. Don't miss out.

Using hides

Hides can give you great views, and are more comfortable and warmer than being completely outside.

When you are in a hide:

● talk quietly

● don't stick your arms out of the windows – this might frighten off any nearby birds

● listen to what other people say they are seeing, then make up your own mind – they might be wrong!

● scan the whole area in front of the hide for birds – don't wait for other people to point them out. Look near to the hide and far away. Look in all directions and watch the sky, too.

Immature starling

Bringing birds closer

You can't always get out and about, or travel, to watch birds. But there are ways you can attract them to your area. If you have a garden, try making it better for birds. There are many things you can do to create your own mini nature reserve.

Feeding

You can make bird feeders or buy them. If you buy one, buy a good one – cheap feeders don't always work that well and don't last any longer than home-made ones. Put the feeders where you can see them easily from the house. To protect feeding birds, don't put feeders too low or anywhere near where cats could hide. Clean the feeders from time to time. Do this outside and wash your hands afterwards. Dirty feeders can spread diseases to visiting birds. Most people use sunflower seeds or special seed mixes in their feeders. Try to buy bird food from a specialist bird food supplier if you can (see page 55).

Greenfinches love sunflower seed. Goldfinches like it too.

Alternatively, you can feed the birds scraps from your home.

Here are some ideas to get you started:

apples; small pieces of bacon rind; cheese; boiled or baked potato; raw pastry; bread; biscuit crumbs; nuts (not salted); and oats (not cooked).

Great tit, nuthatch, robin and great spotted woodpecker. An excellent feeding station.

36

Water

Birds need water for drinking and bathing. A flower pot tray about 30cm across is good for this. Put out water regularly and keep it clean and topped up. A pond is even better and will attract lots of other wildlife too. Make sure it's got some shallow edges.

Right: This woodpigeon is drinking at a pond, but even small areas of water can attract birds.

Left: An immature blue tit checks out the outside world.

Nest sites

Put up nestboxes in your garden. Different designs suit different species – some have holes, others have open fronts. You can buy them or make them. Put nestboxes somewhere safe from cats, ideally where you can watch them from a safe distance.

Face them north or east to avoid overheating the chicks inside in the summer. Blue tits and great tits often nest in nestboxes. Starlings and house sparrows are getting rarer, so you could put up boxes for these too. Nestboxes can be put up at any time of year, but it's best to get them up by the end of January ready for birds to use in spring – if you're lucky!

Gardening

Talk to whoever looks after your garden, or get involved yourself. Investigate plants that are good for wildlife. You will need to find out which species might grow in your garden. Try to grow plants that provide seeds or fruit for birds to eat, plants that attract insects, and plants that provide shelter and nesting places.

TOP TIP

Take a small bag of bird seed with you when you go birding. If you plan to end up where you started, scatter some seed on the ground near the beginning of your walk. When you get back there, have a look to see if any birds are feeding on it. Ask permission before you do this on a nature reserve, farm or country park.

On the spot

Now you've got close to birds, here are some other tips you might find useful.

Pointing out a bird

If you want to show a bird to someone else, you may need to help them find it. Try:

- giving directions from things that are easy to see ("it's below the big tree"; "just to the right of the black and white cow"; "right next to the signpost")

- using the clock method ('it's about 50 metres away at 11 o'clock". See below.)

If you are seawatching (watching birds on or flying over the sea), describing a bird's position can be even harder, especially if it keeps disappearing behind waves. The clock method helps, or you could use these questions to help describe the bird's position:

Go seawatching and you might see a manx shearwater. The shearwater on the right is at 2 o'clock.

- Is the bird flying to the left or the right?

- Is it above or below the horizon?

- How far out is it – halfway out?

- Are there any boats or buoys you can use to help? ("It's flying left, just past the orange buoy.")

Putting birds first

Make sure your bird watching doesn't harm any birds, or upset farmers or other landowners. Remember:

- Birds always come first! Do nothing that might harm them. Disturb them as little as possible.

- Protect habitats. Take care when you are bird watching not to damage the places birds live.

- Don't bird watch on private property unless you know you are allowed to be there.

- Be polite and considerate to other people you meet when you are bird watching.

- Send your bird records to your local bird recorder (see page 41) and put them on BirdTrack (www.birdtrack.net) too.

- Follow the bird protection laws. Contact the RSPB (see page 54) for a free copy of *Birds and the Law*.

Making it count

Your birding can produce information that's useful for conservation – especially if you are the only person watching your local birds. A notebook, or some other form of on-the-spot record, is essential for collecting accurate information. You won't be able to remember everything if you wait until you get home.

Try to note down:

- the birds you saw
- when and where you saw them
- how many you saw
- any interesting behaviour or other observations
- the weather conditions.

Here's an example:

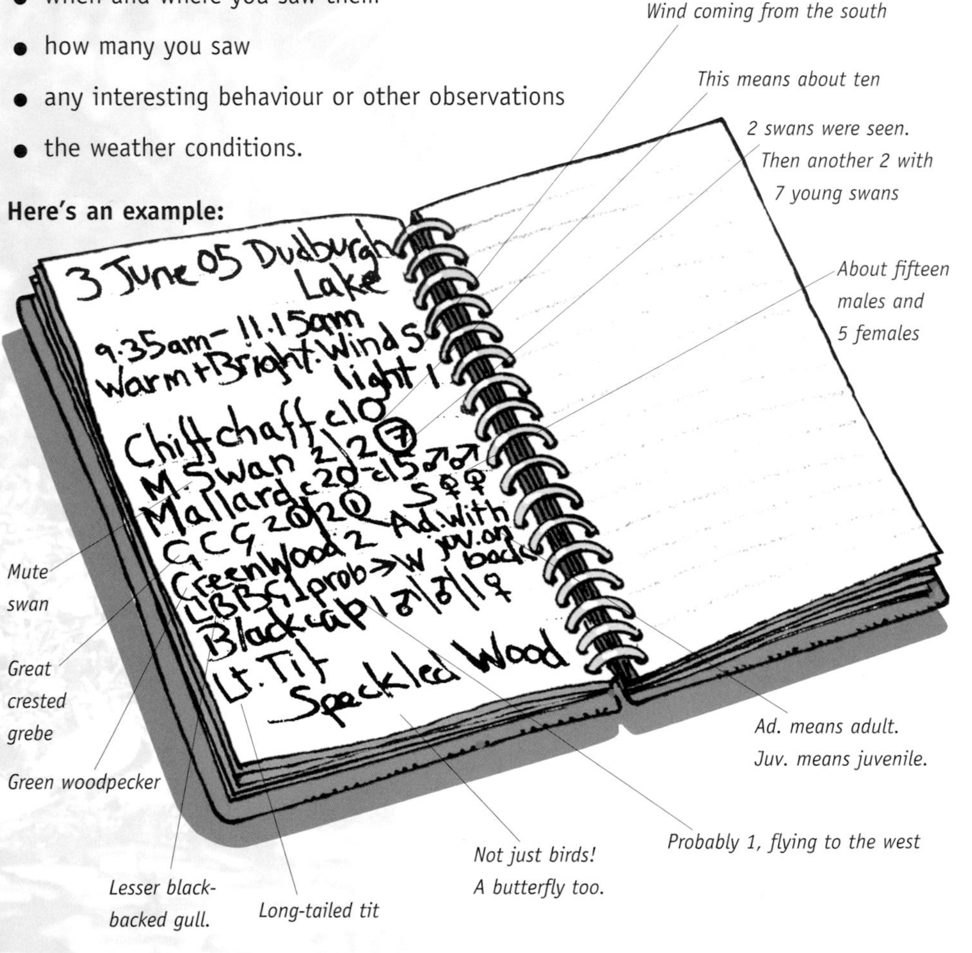

3 June 05 Dudburgh Lake
9.35am–11.15am
Warm + Bright. Wind S light 1
Chiffchaff c10
M.Swan 2/2 ⑦
Mallard c20–c15♂♂ 5♀♀
GCG 2①2①
Green Wood 2 Ad.with juv.on back
LBBG 1 prob → W
Blackcap 1♂/1♂/1♀
Lt.Tit
Speckled Wood
Wind coming from the south
This means about ten
2 swans were seen. Then another 2 with 7 young swans
About fifteen males and 5 females
Mute swan
Great crested grebe
Green woodpecker
Ad. means adult. Juv. means juvenile.
Probably 1, flying to the west
Not just birds! A butterfly too.
Lesser black-backed gull.
Long-tailed tit

To make your information count, you need to send it to the local bird recorder. You

can find out who this is by looking in the Birdwatcher's Yearbook (see page 55) or on one of the birding websites (Fat Birder, for example). Local bird recorders will be particularly interested in anything you see that proves a bird is breeding, or trying to breed. This includes birds singing in the breeding season, birds carrying nesting material, and young birds that have recently left the nest.

Numbers matter

Bird recorders will also be interested in unusually large counts of any species. 'Large' means different things for different species. A flock of 12 Bullfinches might not be difficult to count, but it is a rare enough sight to make it worth telling the recorder.

Some species form much bigger flocks containing hundreds or thousands of birds. These are hard to count – the flock might be flying, or some of the birds might be hidden. You won't get a completely accurate count of a big flock. The aim is to make a good estimate. To do this, count part of the flock – 30 birds, for example. If the flock looks roughly four times bigger than the section you counted, your estimate is 120 birds. If it's roughly seven times bigger, estimate 210 birds. There's another example in the photo below.

20 birds counted. This is about a quarter of the flock so your estimate is 20 x 4 = 80 birds. These are black-tailed godwits.

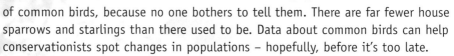

Above and right: Don't forget common birds like house sparrows and blackbirds. Make a note of your counts of these species too.

Ordinary is interesting

Routine records can be important, too. Recorders are sometimes short of records of common birds, because no one bothers to tell them. There are far fewer house sparrows and starlings than there used to be. Data about common birds can help conservationists spot changes in populations – hopefully, before it's too late.

Declare if it's rare

Local recorders will also be interested in any rare birds you see. They will have to be sure that you really did see what you think you saw – they will want to see the notes you made to identify the bird. Part of their job is to make sure that any birds that are recorded are accurately identified.

You can send in your records to local recorders by post or e-mail. Some people send them in once a year, others more often. If you see a rare bird, send in the details as soon as possible. Once a year, a county bird report is published. If you have sent in records, you will probably find your name in it.

TOP TIP

Find out who your local bird recorder is and send in your records. Your observations will be added to a database and may help conserve birds in the future.

You can also make a difference by collecting data for a survey organised by the British Trust for Ornithology (BTO), the RSPB or another conservation body. Here are some things you could try.

Big Garden Birdwatch/Big Schools' Birdwatch
This takes place during the last weekend of January and has been running since 1979. Hundreds of thousands of people take part and it only takes an hour. You can find out more at www.rspb.org.uk, or in RSPB or RSPB Wildlife Explorer magazines.

Birdtrack
A great way to put your bird watching records to good use. It's organised by the BTO, and is all online. You can find out more at www.bto.org/birdtrack

BTO surveys
The BTO organises a range of surveys. Check out www.bto.org for more information.

Nature's calendar
Record information about a range of natural events to observe how climate change is affecting birds. See www.naturescalendar.org.uk

Left: Little egrets are getting commoner. Have they reached your area yet?

Right: A barn owl. Definitely worth telling the bird recorder about!

WARNING

Data can often be submitted online, but you may have to register on some websites. Check with your parents or guardians before you do this.

The birder's year

Here are some suggestions for birding activities throughout the year. You'll need an adult's help for some of them, so use these pages to persuade someone to lend a hand!

January

- Start a year list – a tally of all the bird species you see during the year.

- Listen out for the few birds that sing in winter. Learn their songs before spring when the air is full of bird song and it's much more confusing. Try to learn the songs of the robin, song thrush, mistle thrush, great tit and dunnock (see page 9 to find out how).

*Robin. One of the species to look for in **Big Garden Birdwatch**.*

- Get ready for the **Big Garden Birdwatch** (see page 43) which takes place during the last weekend of January. Feed the birds in your garden and send in your results online if you can. Or, ask your teacher if your class could do **Big Schools' Birdwatch**.

- Look for local feeding flocks of buntings (yellowhammer, reed bunting and sometimes other species), finches and larks (from November to March).

The breeding season has already begun for rooks (below) and mistle thrushes (bottom).

February

- Blackbirds start singing. Learn their song and add it to the list of bird songs you recognise (see page 9).

- If you are putting up nestboxes, get them up by the middle of the month at the latest.

- Watch some early nest-building activity at your nearest rookery (where lots of rooks nest in one place) or heronry (where lots of herons nest together). Mistle thrushes and blackbirds build nests early, too.

- Visit an estuary to see wintering waders and wildfowl. If the coast is too far away, visit an inland wetland to see wintering ducks, geese and swans (November to February).

● This is the month when summer migrants really begin to arrive. Start a list of the dates on which you first see each migrant species. Wheatear, little ringed plover, sand martin, chiffchaff and sandwich tern are among the first. Look out for organisations collecting summer migrant dates, and send them your information. The further north you are, the later the birds will get to you. Watch the sky, too – you might see migrants flying over.

Signs of spring. Wheatears (above) arrive in March, house martins (left), in April.

● Watch your local birds for signs of nesting. They may be carrying nesting material or, later in the month, taking food to the nest.
House sparrows, starlings, blackbirds and collared doves are good ones to watch. You could help out by putting out pet fur, straw and other materials for them to collect.

● Spend time in your local woodland. Use this period before the leaves come out to identify some of the different birds that are singing. Try to learn the songs of the chaffinch, willow warbler, wren, dunnock and blackcap (see page 9).

● Keep watching for migrants arriving.

● Visit a nature reserve that includes several different habitats, ideally on the coast. Look out for summer visitors, birds passing through on migration and lots of breeding activity (from April to May).

● Check out the RSPB's website (see page 55) to discover which **Aren't Birds Brilliant!** sites are open. If you can get to one you could see sspreys, peregrines, puffins or other brilliant species.

Right: Like many birds in April, this puffin is busy nest building.

45

May

● This is baby bird month. Watch your local birds to see how many young the different species have, and what they are eating. The young birds will look different from their parents – more to learn! If you find a baby bird, don't pick it up! Get a *Baby Birds* leaflet from the RSPB. It tells you exactly what to do.

Great crested grebe chicks are stripy and hitch rides on a parent's back.

● Listen to the dawn chorus. Persuade someone to take you to a wood, country park or nature reserve, or just get up early (about 4.00am!), open the window and listen. Do it just before daylight for the best experience – it's early, but worth it!

● Watch out for the last of the summer migrants arriving.

● Visit a heathland at dusk to look and listen for nightjars and woodcock. Or try a wetland for snipe, reed warblers, sedge warblers, grasshopper warblers and more (May to June).

These grey cygnets will be white when they are adult swans.

June

● The breeding season continues – keep an eye on what your local birds are up to.

● Visit a seabird colony – be prepared for lots of birds, noise and smells! You could see puffins, guillemots, razorbills, kittiwakes, fulmars and gannets (from June to July).

● If you get the chance, try birding on moorland or mountains. You could see red grouse, golden plover and curlew (from May to July).

Gannets. Spectacular!

● Some waders are already migrating south. Visit a wetland to look for them – spotted redshank, grey plover, green sandpiper and curlew sandpiper are all possible (from July to August).

● Watch for young birds locally. Juveniles may look different to adults – get to know them.

Above: Green sandpiper. On its way south from its breeding grounds.

● If you're at the coast, look out to sea. You could see migrating seabirds, including skuas and shearwaters. The east, south and south-west coasts are good locations at this time of year.

● Take a birding boat trip for great encounters with skuas, shearwaters, auks and more. There are a few places where boats go to sea, just to look for birds. Some of the best go from Bridlington in Humberside.

Left: Get close to seabirds.
Far left: manx shearwater: a long-lived, long distance traveller.

● Clean your birdfeeders, fill them up and put them out in your garden. Remember, you can feed birds all year round if you want to.

● Watch out for late swifts, young chiffchaffs moving through gardens, and other summer visitors that are starting to head south this month. Look up and you might see flocks of migrating swallows and house martins.

Time to fill up the feeders.

October

• If you have nestboxes, clean them out. They'll be ready for next spring, and some birds might use them to roost in over winter (October to November).

• Migrants are moving. An October day at a nature reserve on the coast can be fantastic, but get there early.

• Look for redwings and fieldfares in your garden, local fields or hedges. These thrushes breed in Scandinavia and spend winter in the UK.

Wintering geese arrive in October. You could see Brent geese or pink-footed geese at the coast.

November

• Find out where your nearest starling roost is and take an early evening look. It could be spectacular.

• Many trees are leafless – use your binoculars to look among the branches for nests that were used earlier in the year.

• Waxwings may begin to arrive – especially in the east. If you hear of any near you, go to see them – they are well worth it. Or, you might be lucky and find your own first.

A starling roost. A lot of birds!

December

• Visit a gull roost towards the end of the afternoon. The big flocks are impressive – and you can practise your gull identification (September to March).

Gulls. Ideal for testing your skills on a cold winter's day!

Use these suggestions to get the most out of your school holidays. Here are things you can do at home, and away from home.

Easter

Look out for:

- signs of breeding
- summer migrants.

Check out:

- a nature reserve with lots of different habitats. One on the coast is best. Visit as late in April as possible – more migrants will be in
- an **Aren't Birds Brilliant!** site. Check the RSPB website (www.rspb.org.uk) for details of when each site opens
- the dawn chorus.

Why not:

- learn how to make your own bird food? Look at the RSPB website for tips.

Summer

Look out for:

- juvenile birds
- butterflies and dragonflies – definitely worth a look!

Check out:

- a coastal wetland
- seawatching
- a birding boat trip
- a seabird colony
- an **Aren't Birds Brilliant!** site.

Why not:

- keep a list of all the birds you see during the holiday?

Christmas

Look out for:

- winter thrushes
- finch, bunting and lark flocks
- feeding flocks in local woodland.

Check out:

- an estuary
- a wildfowl spectacle.

Why not:

- make a nestbox and put it up before the breeding season starts.

Right: Help homeless birds. Build a nestbox.

On your travels

Holidays are a great chance to look for birds in new places. If you are the only birder in your family, take these tips to get some birds into your holiday.

Holidays at home

The UK has lots of holiday destinations with interesting birds nearby. Weymouth in Dorset has an RSPB reserve right next to the railway station. There are excellent views of the Exe estuary from hides at Dawlish Warren in Devon, a nature reserve close to the holidaymakers' beach. In Lancashire, Southport Pier is great for seeing estuary birds, and there are ospreys in the Lake District as well as Scotland.

Norfolk. Good for family holidays, and birds.

All the fun of the fair and birds too. Southport.

These are just a few examples. Do your research before you go – you might be surprised at the possibilities! Check the RSPB's website to see if there's an **Aren't birds brilliant!** site in the area you're visiting.

Some places might interest the rest of the family while providing some birding too. The grounds around historic buildings and stately homes can be good for birds. Most people enjoy boat trips around islands – and these can be great for seeing many kinds of wildlife.

Be prepared

Keep your binoculars with you at all times. You might be surprised. Take care on the beach, though – sand in binoculars is not a good idea, as it can scratch the lenses.

TOP TIP

Try persuading your family that everyone can choose an activity for one or two days of the holiday. Your choice can be a visit to the best birding place in the area!

Holidays abroad can provide exciting introductions to bird species that you have never seen before. There are exciting birds almost everywhere. For example, a holiday in the south of Spain could include bee-eaters, vultures and even flamingoes.

All the tips in this book will work abroad, though the research will be harder. There are site guides ("Where to Watch Birds" books) for many parts of the world. Try these, or see what you can find out on the web. Make sure you have a good field guide for the area too.

Any holiday can include birds. If you stay in a hotel, there may be birds around the hotel's grounds. If you are staying at a busy resort, you could try a walk just outside the resort.

But make sure you go with an adult.

Once you get away from the crowds, there will probably be birds. Don't forget to watch the sea. The Mediterranean Sea, for example, can be a good place to see shearwaters.

Enjoy your holiday!

There are some fantastic birds around the Mediterranean. You could see stripy, crested hoopoes (above top) and colourful bee-eaters (left). The best bit of a holiday in Florida might be diving brown pelicans (above centre)!

51

Taking it further

If you've read this far, this book won't be enough! There are many things you can do to take your interest further. Here are some ideas:

Join up

RSPB Wildlife Explorers is the junior membership of the RSPB. Join and take part in competitions, events, projects and even holidays. There are local groups where you can meet other young people who are into birds and wildlife. And you get six magazines a year too. Find out more at: www.rspb.org.uk/youth

Making birdcake. Wildlife Explorer groups don't just watch birds.

Get a magazine

Bird Watching magazine is good to start with. It comes out once a month and is full of articles about birds and birding. For something more advanced, try *Birdwatch*.

Explore the web

There are lots of bird watching websites. Try the ones on the right first, or see if your local bird club has one. Always make sure a grown-up knows what you're doing when you're online.

WEBSITES TO VISIT

RSPB youth pages
www.rspb.org.uk/youth

Fat Birder
www.fatbirder.com

Get a telescope

For really great views of birds, far away or close up, invest in a telescope. You will also need a good tripod to put it on. A magnification of 20–30x is plenty for most situations. The views can be good, but it can be awkward carrying the equipment. Do

your research before you buy. Watch the birding magazines for reviews. Buy from a specialist shop and hunt for second-hand bargains. A good telescope doesn't have to be too expensive.

Make it big! Try to look through a friend's telescope if you don't have your own.

Start digiscoping

Put a digital camera over the eyepiece of a telescope and you can take great pictures of birds. Many 'digiscopers' use special adaptors to hold the camera in the right position over the eyepiece. It will take practice to get good pictures, but any pictures you take might help you identify a bird later. Some digiscopers put their pictures on the web. This means that other people can see the bird on their computer very soon after the bird was sighted for real.

Become a ringer

Ringers catch birds and put lightweight rings on their legs to find out more about bird movements and how long birds live. Seeing a bird in the hand is an amazing experience. The BTO organises bird ringing in the UK and they want more young ringers. It takes years of training to learn the skills to become fully licensed, so you will need to be very keen and committed. To find out more, contact the BTO (see page 54).

Find out more about ringing at www.bto.org/ringing

53

Useful information

Organisations

RSPB Wildlife Explorers
The Lodge
Sandy
Beds SG19 2DL
Tel: 01767 680551
www.rspb.org.uk/youth

British Trust for Ornithology (BTO)
The National Centre for Ornithology
The Nunnery
Thetford
Norfolk IP24 2PU
Tel: 01842 750050
www.bto.org

Wildfowl and Wetlands Trust
Slimbridge
Gloucestershire GL2 7BT
Tel: 01453 891900
www.wwt.org.uk

The Wildlife Trusts (and Wildlife Watch)
The Kiln
Waterside
Mather Road
Newark
Nottinghamshire NG24 1WT
Tel: 0870 0367711
www.wildlifetrusts.org

Robin

Books

The BTO Nestbox Guide
By Chris Du Feu and Derek Toomer
BTO, 2003

RSPB Pocket Birdfeeder Guide
By Robert Burton
Dorling Kindersley, 2004

Kingfisher

The Bird-friendly Garden
By Stephen Moss
Harper Collins, 2004

The Birdwatcher's Yearbook
Buckingham Press
55 Thorpe Park Road
Peterborough PE3 6LJ
Tel: 01733 561739

Skylark

Great tit

Multimedia

WildSounds: www.wildsounds.co.uk

Birdguides: www.birdguides.com

Other websites

BirdLife International: www.birdlife.org

**Bird Links to the World:
www.bsc- eoc.org/links**

Fat Birder: www.fatbirder.com

RSPB: www.rspb.org.uk

Surfbirds: www.surfbirds.com

Bird food and feeding suppliers

RSPB Sales Ltd: www.rspbshop.co.uk

CJ WildBird foods: www.birdfood.co.uk

The field guide

This short field guide (pages 56–125) will help you to identify most birds that you might see in the UK and Ireland. Look at the pictures and read the descriptions carefully. Make a note of where and when you saw the bird, and what it was doing. It is often best to start by ruling out what the bird is not.

Pictures

The pictures show each bird's shape, colour and markings, and the way it perches or flies. They also show any important differences between male and female or between breeding and non-breeding plumage. Beware: birds don't always look like their picture! A pale bird looks dark with the sun behind it. A slim bird can look fat in cold weather.

Descriptions

The first piece of information about each bird is its name and length. Be careful: these can sometimes be misleading. For instance, a common gull is not as 'common' as some other gulls. A magpie's long tail makes it the same length as a carrion crow, even though it is really a smaller bird (see page 6).

Simple icons help you to find the key information about each bird and to make quick comparisons between different species. The box below explains what each one means.

IDENTIFICATION		*This tells you what the bird looks like: its size, shape, colours and markings. 'Summer' refers to breeding plumage (roughly March to July, for most birds); 'winter' refers to non-breeding plumage (the rest of the year).*
BEHAVIOUR		*This tells you what the bird does – how it moves and feeds, whether it lives alone or in groups and any unusual habits it has.*
VOICE		*This tells you what noises the bird makes, including its songs and calls.*
WHERE TO SEE		*This tells you roughly where the bird lives and what kind of habitat it prefers. It also tells you when you are likely to see each species, and how common it is.*
DON'T CONFUSE WITH		*This lists other birds that look like the bird being described. Some might be from a different family (for instance, Swifts look a bit like Swallows, but are not related to them). Not all of them appear in this book, so you may have to look at other field guides too.*

♂ : male   ♀ : female   I : immature (non-adult plumage)

Little Grebe (25–29cm)

This is the smallest bird that swims on fresh water.

summer

winter

 small size; dumpy shape with **fluffy rear end**; brown all over; reddish neck and cheeks in summer; paler in winter; bare patches at base of hill

dives often (and often re-surfaces out of sight); rivals chase each other over water, half running/half flying; young often ride on parents' backs; gathers in small groups during winter

loud, high-pitched trill

common, but can be hard to see; breeds on ponds, canals and slow-flowing rivers; moves to larger lakes in winter

slavonian grebe, black-necked grebe, young moorhen or coot

Great Crested Grebe (46–51cm)

This large, slim grebe sports fancy summer headgear.

slightly smaller than mallard, with long neck and pointed bill; white underneath and brown above; in summer, **shaggy ruff on cheeks**; in winter, white and grey; white wing markings in flight

dives often; rests head on back; rarely flies; pairs perform dancing courtship displays in spring; gathers in small groups during winter

mostly silent

common, except for northern Scotland; breeds on inland waters – often in towns; in winter, moves to larger lakes, reservoirs and sea

red-necked grebe, goosander, red-breasted merganser, young cormorant or shag

winter

summer

Fulmar (45–50cm)

This seabird's stiff-winged flight shows that it is not a gull.

similar to medium-sized gull, but with shorter neck, stubbier bill and **straighter, narrower wings**; white, with mottled grey wings and dark eye

glides smoothly along cliffs or low over water, with short bursts of flapping; nests in small colonies on cliffs; sometimes perches on sea

cackling at nest

breeds on cliffs all round coast; hardly ever seen inland; travels far out to sea.

medium-sized gulls, manx shearwater

SECRET WEAPON

The fulmar produces special oil in its stomach to feed its chicks. It can squirt this oil at any intruder that gets too close to the nest. The oil makes such a sticky, stinky mess that the intruder quickly backs off.

Gannet (87–100cm)

This huge, white seabird dives from high up to catch fish.

bigger than any gull, with long body, pointed wings and tail, and dagger-like bill; adult has **snow-white plumage, black wing tips and yellowish head;** young are grey-brown all over

straight flight, with heavy flaps and long glides; when fishing, circles above sea and plunges in with a splash; flocks fish together; often sits on water

cackling at nest

breeds in big sea-cliff colonies in north and west; travels huge distances during winter and may be seen anywhere offshore

large gulls, large shearwaters

Diving for fish

Cormorant (80–100cm)

This large, dark water bird catches fish by diving from the surface.

long body and long, thick neck; powerful bill with hooked tip; **adult is black, with white patch on face and thigh in summer;** young are brown above and pale below

sits low in water with bill tilted upwards; dives with small leap; flies very straight, sometimes high up; likes to perch on sandbanks or jetties, often with wings outstretched

croaks and growls at nest

common in inland and coastal waters, including towns and cities; breeds in colonies on sea cliffs or trees beside lakes

shag, divers, larger grebes, goosander, red-breasted merganser

Shag (65–80cm)

Look closely: a 'cormorant' on a rocky coast may be a shag.

similar to cormorant, but smaller, with thinner bill; blackish-green all over in summer, with small crest on forehead; young are brown, and paler below.

fishes just like Cormorant, but leaps forward more when diving; flies low over water; perches only on rocks – often with wings outstretched

grunting noises at nest

breeds on rocky coasts around north and west; nests low down on cliffs; likes rough water around rocks; seldom seen inland

cormorant, divers, larger grebes, goosander, red-breasted merganser

OTHER BIRDS AT SEA

You can often see many other birds on the sea, especially during winter and migration times. Here are a few to look out for.

Long-tailed duck
Black and white sea duck; male has long tail.

Common scoter
All-dark sea duck; often in large flocks

Eider
Plump sea duck; breeding male is black and white

Great skua
Big and dark; white wing patches; chases other birds

Red-breasted merganser
Slim, long-billed sea duck; dives often

Red-throated diver
Smallest, commonest diver; pale in winter

Manx shearwater
Dark above, white below; stiff-winged flight over waves

Grey Heron (90–98cm)

A heron stands taller than any other water bird.

 very tall, with long legs, long, thin neck and dagger-shaped bill; broad, rounded wings; mostly grey, with black and white markings; young are greyer all over

usually solitary; stands in shallow water with neck kinked, waiting to grab fish or frogs; rests hunched up; flies with slow wingbeats, neck drawn up and legs trailing

deep croak in flight

common on still inland waters and sheltered coasts; visits garden ponds for goldfish; breeds in large colonies in tall trees

bittern, large gulls or large birds of prey (in flight)

Little Egret (55–65cm)

This all-white heron often chases its prey through the shallows.

heron-shaped, but much smaller and **pure white all over**; black bill, black legs with yellow feet; rounded wings

usually solitary; always feeds in water; stands waiting for prey or chases it through shallow water with wings raised; flies with neck drawn up and legs trailing; roosts and breeds in trees beside water

usually silent, except at breeding colonies

southern parts of the UK on estuaries and marshes; gathers along coast in winter

gulls or barn owl (in flight)

Mute Swan (125–155 cm)

This enormous, white waterfowl is Britain's largest bird.

huge, with very long neck; adults are **all-white with orange-and-black bill**; young are dirty brown

usually seen swimming in pairs or small groups; often holds folded wings raised; runs along surface to get airborne; wings make loud, whooshing sound in flight; can be aggressive

hisses when angry

common on inland waters, such as ponds, lakes and slow-flowing rivers; also in estuaries; the only Swan likely to be seen in towns

whooper and bewick's swan (winter only), white farmyard geese

FEATHER RECORD

Swans have more feathers on their body than any other bird. A mute swan has about 25,000 in total, of which over 80 per cent are on its head and neck.

Greylag Goose (75–90 cm)

This common 'grey goose' is the ancestor of most domestic geese.

large, fat goose, with long neck, orange bill and pink legs; greyish-brown plumage with white under tail; shows pale grey forewing and underwing in flight

usually in flocks on or beside water; often grazes on farmland; flocks fly in straggly 'V' formations

noisy cackling and honking – especially in flight

widespread on inland waters, estuaries and marshes; 'true' wild greylags breed only in northern Scotland, but feral birds are widespread; more common in winter.

pink-footed goose, white-fronted goose, bean goose

Pink-footed goose: *smaller and darker than greylag, with small head, pink-and-black bill, pink legs and no grey on wings; flocks visit coastal marshes in winter.*

Canada Goose (56–110cm)

This big, black-necked goose is a common sight in towns and parks.

taller and longer-necked than other geese, though varies greatly in size; brown body, with pale breast and white under tail; black head and neck with **white patch on cheeks**; black bill and legs

usually in flocks on water, or grazing on nearby grass; can upend to feed in deeper water; flocks fly in loose formation; often roosts on water

loud trumpeting

common, except for northern Scotland; prefers lowland inland waters – including reservoirs and city lakes

Brent goose, barnacle goose

Brent goose: *smaller and darker than Canada goose, with short bill and (in adults) white mark on side of black neck; winter visitor in large flocks to muddy estuaries.*

Shelduck (58–67cm)

A big, mostly white duck on an estuary is probably a shelduck.

larger than mallard; **white, with greenish-black head and neck**, chestnut band around breast, and black wing markings; pink feet and red bill (knob on male's bill)

usually in pairs or family groups; swims and wades while feeding; sweeps bill through mud to sift small food; often nests in burrows

males are usually silent; female has low, growling call

all around coast, though less common in Scotland; prefers estuaries with mudflats and sandbanks; uncommon inland

male shoveler, male eider

♂

Wigeon (45–51cm)

You often see (and hear!) this duck in large flocks.

- slightly smaller than mallard, with shorter neck and bill; male has grey body, **chestnut head, yellow forehead and white stripe on side**, with conspicuous white wing-patches in flight; female is brown, with white belly

- gathers in winter to graze on waterside grasses; also feeds in water; takes off in large flocks

- male has high-pitched whistle – *whee-ooo*; flocks often call together

- winter visitor to wetlands and coastal marshes; also lakes, reservoirs and gravel pits inland; small numbers breed in Scotland and northern England

- teal, mallard, pochard.

Teal (34–38cm)

Don't miss this little duck feeding quietly by the water's edge.

- half the size of mallard; male has chestnut head with dark green eye-patch, grey body with white stripe along flank and **yellow patch under tail**; female is brown and speckled, like small female mallard

- feeds quietly in pairs or small groups; often upends; takes off vertically when alarmed and flies away very fast

- male makes short, high-pitched whistle

- widespread and common in winter; in summer, small numbers breed in quiet areas; prefers marshland and small patches of shallow water

- mallard, wigeon

64

Mallard (50–65cm)

This common duck is a familiar sight all over the world.

♀

♂

large duck with long bill; male is pale grey with **bottle-green head and white neck ring**, purplish breast, curly tail feathers and yellow bill; female is speckled brown with dark eye-stripe and orange bill; many domestic varieties

usually seen in pairs or small groups; often very tame; feeds by dipping head and neck underwater or upending

female makes typical duck quacking; male is quieter

on fresh water anywhere, from village ponds to coastal marshes; in winter sometimes also at sea

gadwall, teal, wigeon

Gadwall (45–56cm)

This medium-sized duck is more common than many people realise.

similar shape to mallard, but slightly smaller; male is **greyish-brown with black rear end**; female is like a slimmer, greyer female mallard, with orange sides to bill; both sexes have white wing-patch which shows well in flight

feeds on the water's surface in pairs or small groups; often sits quietly at the water's edge

usually silent: female makes a high-pitched quack; male croaks in flight

most common in southern and eastern England; more widespread in winter; prefers large areas of water, including lakes and reservoirs

mallard

♀

♂

Shoveler (44–52cm)

Inside a shoveler's long bill is a special sieve for filtering food.

 smaller than mallard, with **long bill flattened like shovel**; male has greenish-black head and white underparts, with chestnut patch on flanks; female is speckled brown all over; in flight both show blue wing markings and have front-heavy shape

usually seen feeding on water in pairs or small groups; bill touches surface when feeding; often sits quietly at water's edge

mostly silent

common and widespread, except northern Scotland; breeds on inland and coastal marshes; visits larger inland waters during winter

shelduck (male), mallard (female)

♀

♂

Pintail (51–66cm)

No other freshwater duck has such a long pointed tail.

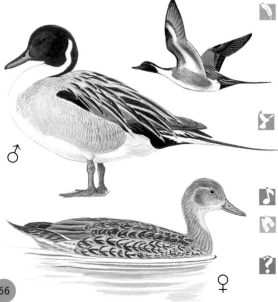

mallard-sized, but slimmer; male is mostly white-and-grey, with chocolate-brown head, **white stripe on neck and long, pointed black tail**; female is speckled brown like female mallard, but with more pointed tail and no eye-stripe

usually seen feeding on water, in pairs or small groups; often upends to reach food deep down with its long neck; flocks fly high in 'V' formation

mostly silent

a rare breeding bird, but widespread in winter on marshy and coastal areas

mallard (female)

♂

♀

Tufted Duck (40–47cm)

This black-and-white diving duck is common in built-up areas.

♂

♀

Goldeneye: *black-and-white, like Tufted Duck, but with puffed-up-looking head; male has white breast and white patch on face; mostly winter visitor to inland waters and coasts*

small diving duck; yellow eyes and blue-grey bill; male is glossy black with pure white flanks and **drooping crest**; female is dark brown with paler flanks and short crest; white wing-bars in flight

usually seen on the water; dives constantly for food; patters across surface to take off; can become tame in town parks

mostly silent

widespread and common on lakes, gravel pits and other inland waters; large flocks gather in winter

goldeneye, pochard (female), scaup (female)

Pochard (42–49cm)

You can often see this dumpy diving duck alongside Tufted Ducks.

small, plump diving duck with rounded head and flat tail; male is **pale grey with reddish head and neck**, and black breast and tail; female is brown and grey; in flight, shows pale grey wing-bars.

dives for food from surface; regularly sleeps on water; runs to take off – like tufted duck

mostly silent

widespread on lakes, gravel pits and other inland waters; uncommon breeding bird, but common in winter when large flocks gather; often visits town parks

tufted duck (female), goldeneye (female), wigeon (male), scaup (female)

♂

♀

Red Kite (60–66cm)

This big, angular bird of prey twists its forked tail in flight.

 bigger than buzzard, with longer wings and **long, forked tail**; reddish-brown body and reddish-orange tail; pale head and pale 'windows' in underwings

soars over open country looking for food; eats mostly dead animals; may gather in small groups to roost or feed

high-pitched *pee-ooo-eee*, similar to buzzard

once nested only in Wales but now becoming more common in parts of England and Scotland; likes farmland with scattered woodland

buzzard, harriers, osprey

COMING HOME

Red kites were confined to Wales for many years. But in 1989, scientists began to reintroduce them to places where they had lived centuries earlier. Now you can also see Red Kites in many parts of England and Scotland.

Buzzard (51–57cm)

You may hear a buzzard's call before you spot it soaring high overhea

big and stocky, with **broad, rounded wings**; brownish all over, but varies from dark to pale; wings show fingers and pale 'windows' underneath

soars high, with wings held in shallow 'V'; hunts small mammals such as rabbits; may hover, but looks clumsy compared to kestrel; perches on fence posts and sometimes in fields

high-pitched, far-carrying *pee-uuuu*

widespread; most common in north and west; likes hilly country with scattered woodland; travels widely during winter

red kite, golden eagle, harriers, rough-legged buzzard, honey buzzard

Kestrel (32–35cm)

Except for quivering wings, a hovering kestrel hangs perfectly still.

 small falcon, with **long tail and pointed wings**; male has spotted, reddish-brown back, grey head and tail, and pale, spotted underparts; female is brown with black markings; both have black band at tip of tail

hunts in the open; hovers above ground then drops onto prey, including rodents and large insects; perches on posts, telegraph wires and other obvious places

shrill *ki-ki-ki-ki-ki*

common, but declining; likes open areas with rough grassland – including motorway verges; nests in towns but seldom visits gardens

sparrowhawk, hobby, merlin, cuckoo

Sparrowhawk (28–38cm)

You may only glimpse this dashing hunter as it shoots past.

small and upright, with **long tail and short, broad wings**; white eyebrow gives fierce expression; male is grey above with reddish barring below; female is much bigger, brown above and barred below

secretive; flies fast and low with 'flap-flap-flap-glide' pattern; catches small birds in flight; on sunny days, soars high – often in circles – with wings and tail spread; uses hidden perches

chattering *kew-kew-kew* when nesting

common and increasing; nests in forests but often hunts in open country; often visits towns, cities and gardens

kestrel, goshawk, cuckoo

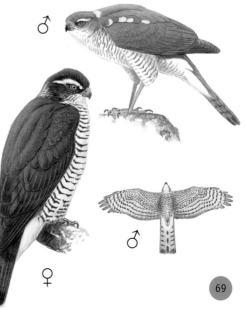

Peregrine Falcon (36–48cm)

This powerful falcon is the jet fighter of the bird world.

- medium-sized with heavy body, shortish tail and broad-based, pointed wings; adults are blue-grey above, with **black head, white throat and cheeks, and black 'moustache'**; adults are barred below, young are streaked

- hunts birds in flight; often dives ('stoops') onto prey from great height; flies fast with quick wingbeats or circles high up; perches on cliffs and tall buildings

- harsh, cackling *kek-rek-rek* when nesting

- breeds in hilly areas of north and west and on rocky sea-cliffs; rare, but increasing; visits lowland areas in winter; may nest on tall buildings

- kestrel, hobby, merlin, woodpigeon

> **SPEED KING**
>
> *A diving peregrine is probably the fastest bird in the world. Scientists think it can reach a speed of 240kph (150mph). But other birds may be faster than peregrines in level flight – including the eider duck, timed at 75kph (47mph).*

Hobby (30–36cm)

Even dragonflies are on the menu for this agile falcon.

- kestrel-sized, but with shorter tail and longer, more pointed wings; adults are blue-grey above, with black head, white throat and cheeks, and black 'moustache' (like peregrine); streaked below (unlike adult peregrine); **red on thighs and under tail**

- hunts small birds and large insects in flight, often over water; may eat small prey in midair; often perches in isolated pine trees

- shrill *kew-kew-kew* when nesting

- uncommon summer visitor to England – especially south-east; also eastern Wales and southern Scotland; nests on lowland heaths and farmland with patches of trees

- kestrel, peregrine, cuckoo

BIRDS OF PREY IN FLIGHT

You will often see flying birds of prey from a distance. Look for their wing shape and any special markings to help identify them.

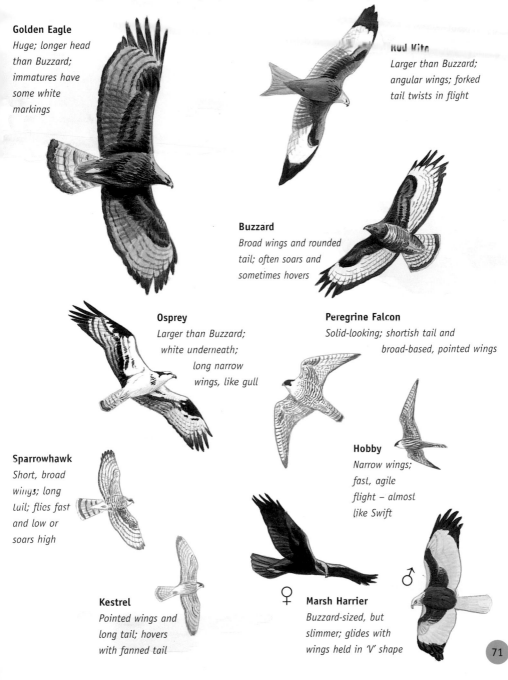

Golden Eagle
Huge; longer head than Buzzard; immatures have some white markings

Red Kite
Larger than Buzzard; angular wings; forked tail twists in flight

Buzzard
Broad wings and rounded tail; often soars and sometimes hovers

Osprey
Larger than Buzzard; white underneath; long narrow wings, like gull

Peregrine Falcon
Solid-looking; shortish tail and broad-based, pointed wings

Sparrowhawk
Short, broad wings; long tail; flies fast and low or soars high

Hobby
Narrow wings; fast, agile flight – almost like Swift

Kestrel
Pointed wings and long tail; hovers with fanned tail

♀ **Marsh Harrier**
Buzzard-sized, but slimmer; glides with wings held in 'V' shape ♂

Red Grouse (37–42cm)

You might disturb this game bird when tramping across moorland.

🔽 bigger than partridge; plump, with short tail and small head; **mottled reddish-brown** all over (hard to spot against heather); pale, feathered legs; male has bright red wattle over eye

🔀 lives on ground in pairs or small groups; when flushed, flies fast and low with whirring wings and long glides

🎵 raucous call sounds like 'go back, go back!'; usually calls when flushed

🌍 upland areas of north and west; heather moorland away from trees

❓ female pheasant, partridges, ptarmigan, black grouse, capercaillie

Pheasant (53–89cm)

This colourful bird was introduced from Asia over 1,000 years ago.

♀

♂

🔽 large, with long neck; male is very colourful, with bottle-green head, bare, red face, copper underparts and **long, barred, orange tail**; some males have white neck-ring; female is pale brown with shorter (but still long) tail

🔀 walks slowly and deliberately; runs when disturbed, or takes off with explosion of wingbeats; flies low with whirring wings and long glides; roosts in bushes

🎵 raucous *ko-kok* call, while flapping wings

🌍 common on farmland and woodland edges, except in Scottish highlands; thousands are bred and released for hunting

❓ partridges, grouse, golden pheasant

Grey Partridge (29–31cm)

This plump game bird is hard to spot as it crouches in a field.

 small and hunched, with short neck; brown above and grey below, with unmarked, **orange face**; dark brown mark on belly (can be hard to see); reddish tail in flight

lives on ground in small groups; scratches for food with feet; prefers to crouch rather than fly; fast, low flight with whirring wings and long glides

grating *kerrick* call, especially at dusk

widespread, but not in hilly areas of north and west; open grassland and farmland with rough pasture and thick hedges

female pheasant, young red-legged partridge, corncrake, quail

CLUTCH CONTROL

The Grey Partridge lays one of the largest clutches of any bird in the world. It averages 15–19 eggs, but may even top 25. A female sometimes lays more than one clutch per season, in which case her second clutch is smaller.

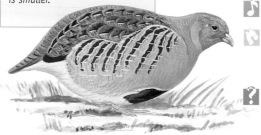

Red-legged Partridge (32–34cm)

This colourful partridge is easier to spot than its grey cousin.

slightly larger and less hunched than grey partridge; brown-and-grey plumage; **white throat-patch with black border**; black 'necklace' on breast; bold bars on flanks

feeds more out in open than grey partridge, and often in larger group; perches on vantage points such as posts; picks and scratches for food; runs when disturbed; flies like grey partridge

loud *chuck-chukka-chuck* call

common in southern, central and eastern England; also eastern Scotland and eastern Northern Ireland; open, dry farmland and woodland edges

female pheasant, grey partridge, corncrake, quail

Moorhen (32–35cm)

Look for a moorhen chugging around the edge of a pond.

 smallish, plump water bird with up-tilted tail; dark brown and smoky grey, but looks black from a distance; **white line along flank and white under tail**; red forehead and red bill with yellow tip; young are pale below; long toes dangle in flight

 feeds on land and water, often near bank; usually alone or in small groups; swims with nodding head and flicking tail

♪ loud *krruuuk* call

common, except in hilly areas and north-west Scotland; lakes, ponds, ditches and slow-flowing rivers

❓ coot, little grebe (young)

Coot (36–38cm)

Look out for this dumpy, black water bird on almost any large lake.

larger than moorhen, with rounder shape and shorter tail; **sooty black, with white bill and forehead**; young is pale below; long toes dangle in flight

feeds mostly on water, often among other water birds; dives often; also feeds on bank; sometimes forms large flocks; quarrelsome – fights and chases rivals

♪ loud *kowk* call

common, except in hilly areas and north-west Scotland; large open bodies of fresh water, such as park lakes and reservoirs

❓ moorhen, tufted duck, grebes (young)

Oystercatcher (40–45cm)

This big, black-and-white wader is a noisy seaside resident.

large, stocky wader; black head, neck and upperparts, white underparts; white chin-strap in winter; **long, orange bill and pink legs;** in flight white rump and wing-bars

Noisy and obvious; often flies about while calling; feeds along shore on shellfish, but doesn't wade deeply; also eats worms in fields; forms large flocks in winter

loud, high-pitched, piping *peep peep peep*

common all around coast; in northern regions also inland along river valleys; gathers in estuaries in winter

avocet, lapwing

Avocet (42–45cm)

This slim, elegant wader is our only bird with a fully upturned bill.

Oystercatcher-sized, but much slimmer, with longer neck and legs; mostly white, with black on crown, back of neck and back; **thin, upturned bill;** blueish legs; looks mostly white in flight

wades in shallow water; feeds by sweeping bill from side to side; often upends, may swim; very excitable – chases rivals and other birds; flocks in winter

piping *klute klute* call when alarmed

increasing – breeds in shallow coastal lagoons along coast of southern and south-eastern England; winters in south-west England

oystercatcher, gulls (in flight), black-winged stilt (rare)

75

Lapwing (28–31cm)

This colourful, noisy plover is most at home in fields and meadows.

 dove-sized, with long legs, short bill and **long crest**; dark green above and white below, with black markings on face and breast; broad, rounded wings, with pale wing-tips and white rump; flocks in flight flicker black and white

feeds on land with 'stop-run-peck' action; acrobatic flyer – dives and rolls during courtship display; mobs raptors and other birds; forms large winter flocks

loud, rolling *peewit* call

widespread on farmland and marshy areas; in winter on ploughed fields and along coast; breeding numbers are falling

oystercatcher

Ringed Plover (18–20cm)

Check the tideline carefully for hidden ringed plovers.

FOOLED YOU!

Nesting Ringed Plovers use a trick called a 'distraction display' to fool predators that get too close. The plover limps away as though injured, dragging its wing and calling. The predator follows the adult, and so misses the nest.

small, plump wader with long legs and short bill; white below and sandy brown above; **black band around chest and across face** (fading to brown in winter); orange legs and black-tipped orange bill; narrow, white wing-bars in flight

usually alone or among groups of other small waders; feeds with 'stop-run-peck' action; freezes against background; fast, direct flight

two-note whistle, *too-lip* – usually in flight

common all around coast except south-west; sand and shingle beaches; uncommon inland

little ringed plover, sanderling

Little Ringed Plover: Like Ringed Plover, with yellow eye-ring and no wing-bar; inland summer visitor; passage visitor on coast.

Grey Plover (27–30cm)

Scan carefully across an estuary: you can often spot a grey plover.

winter

 solid shape with long legs and short bill; in winter, grey above and pale below with dark eye; in summer (rare in UK and Ireland), black face and belly; **in flight, black 'armpits' below**, white wing-bar and rump above

feeds alone or widely scattered, with typical plover 'stop-run-peck' action; often freezes; fast, direct flight

sorrowful whistle, *pee-uu-eee* – usually in flight

widespread around coast from autumn to spring, except in parts of northern Scotland and western Ireland; muddy and sandy shores; doesn't breed in UK

golden plover, knot, black-headed gull (winter)

Golden Plover (26–29cm)

Look for this quiet bird among winter flocks of lapwings.

 slimmer than grey plover, with finer bill; in summer, has **yellowish-brown back**, blackish underparts and broad, white line between; in winter, brownish breast and upperparts, and white belly; thin, white wing-bar in flight, but no black armpits

feeds on ground with typical plover 'stop-run-peck' action; forms large flocks – often with lapwings; fast, direct flight

two-note whistle, pu-wee – usually in flight

uncommon breeding bird in boggy, upland regions of north and west; more widespread in winter, when large flocks gather on farmland and coastal marshes.

grey plover

winter

summer

77

Knot (23–25cm)

If you see one knot, you'll probably see hundreds.

 bigger than dunlin, with shortish, straight bill; **greyish in winter**, with white belly and eyebrow; in summer (rare in UK and Ireland), brick-red below, with mottled black-and-grey back; white wing-bar in flight

 forms huge flocks (sometimes in thousands), which twist and turn in flight like shoals of fish; probes in mud for small shellfish

soft *wutt-wutt* flight call

winter and passage visitor to large estuaries and mudflats; uncommon inland; does not breed in UK

redshank, dunlin, grey plover

Flock in flight

winter

Sanderling (20–21cm)

This dinky little wader races along the beach like a clockwork toy.

NORTHERN NESTERS

Knot and sanderling are among many waders that breed in the Arctic. This is why we seldom see their breeding colours or hear them singing. After breeding, they head south for winter. Some stay in the UK, but many travel much further – reaching South Africa, or even Australia.

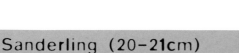

winter

small, hunched wader with short, straight bill; in winter, **white with grey back and dark mark on shoulder**; in summer (rare in UK and Ireland), reddish-brown breast and head and mottled back; in flight, white wing-bar and white sides to rump

very energetic; small parties follow retreating waves to pick food from wet sand

liquid whistle – *twick twick* – in flight

winter and passage visitor to sandy beaches; rare on rocky coasts (including Scotland and south-west England); does not breed in UK

dunlin, knot, ringed plover

Dunlin (16–20cm)

This little wader is often the most numerous in a mixed flock.

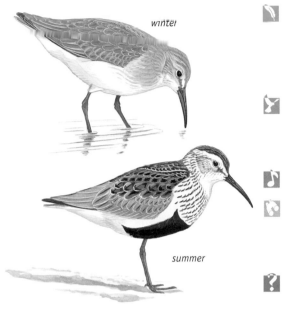

winter

summer

- sparrow-sized, with **slightly downcurved bill**; in winter, brownish-grey above and white below; in summer, reddish brown back and black patch on belly; in flight, white wing-bar and white sides to rump

- may gather in huge flocks – often with other waders; flocks twist and turn in flight; probes mud and wades in shallow water

- short, grating flight call – *kreeet*

- in winter, common all round coast on muddy shores; in summer, smaller numbers breed on boggy upland areas in north and west; inland on passage

- sanderling, knot, curlew sandpiper, purple sandpiper

Turnstone (22–24cm)

Elaborate markings camouflage this chunky wader against the rocks.

- starling-sized wader with short, thick bill and orange legs; in summer, bold black and white pattern on face and breast, and black-and-orange pattern on back; in winter, mottled brown; **black, white and brown pattern striking in flight**

- small groups feed busily at water's edge, turning stones or seaweed; perches on posts; can be very tame

- chuckling *tuk-a-tuk-tuk* call in flight

- common around coast; prefers shores with rockpools and seaweed; does not breed in UK or Ireland; rare inland

- ringed plover, oystercatcher (in flight)

summer

winter

Curlew (50–60cm)

The lonely call of the curlew drifts across estuaries all year round.

 very big, gull-sized wader, with long neck and **very long, down-curved bill**; streaked greyish-brown all over; white rump and back in flight

feeds alone or in scattered groups; probes mud deeply; flocks at high-tide roost – often in fields; fluttering spring display flight, with long glides; looks a bit like gull in flight

lonely, rising *courleee* call; bubbling calls during display

common around coast in winter; in summer, breeds on upland areas in north and west – also on boggy lowland heaths in south

whimbrel, godwits, young gulls

> **TooLS of THE TRADE**
>
> *Each type of wader has a bill suited to its own particular diet. This allows different species to feed together without competition. A dunlin's short bill grabs small creatures near the water surface; a curlew's long bill probes deep into mud for lugworms.*

Bar-tailed Godwit (37–39cm)

You won't often see this wader's rich breeding colours in the UK.

large (but smaller than curlew), with long neck and **long, slightly upturned bill**; in winter, greyish-brown above and pale below; in summer (rare in UK and Ireland), male has brick-red underparts; in flight, white rump and barred tail, but no wing-bars

usually feeds in small flocks, wading and probing mud; larger flocks at high-tide roost, often with other waders

low *kiruk, kiruk* call in flight

in winter, all around coast – though less common in south; prefers muddy shores and estuaries; does not breed in UK or Ireland

black-tailed godwit, curlew, whimbrel, greenshank, spotted redshank

Black-tailed Godwit: *longer legs and straighter bill than Bar-tailed; plainer grey in winter; in flight, black-and-white wings and black tail; winter visitor and rare breeder*

Redshank (27–29cm)

This noisy wader is often first to spot danger and sound the alarm.

summer

winter

medium-sized, with medium-length bill and red legs; speckled brownish in summer, greyer in winter; in flight, white rump and back, and **broad, white band along rear edge of wing**

feeds alone or in small flocks; runs, wades and may swim; quickly takes flight when alarmed; often perches on posts; fluttering spring display flight; raises wings upon landing

ringing *teeu-tu-tu* alarm call; also yodelling lew-lew-lew during display

common on estuaries and salt marshes; also inland on marshes and moorland

greenshank, spotted redshank, green sandpiper, wood sandpiper, ruff

Greenshank (30–33cm)

Look for this elegant wader feeding busily at the back of a pool.

larger, slimmer and paler than redshank, with **long neck, greenish legs and slightly upturned bill**; grey above and white below, with bolder markings in summer; in flight, white rump and back but no white on wings

usually feeds alone; walks fast, wades deeply and may swim; probes mud; sweeps bill from side to side like avocet; fast, twisting flight

ringing three-part *tew-tew-tew* flight call

widespread but uncommon passage migrant to lakes, reservoirs and estuaries; breeds in northern Scotland on peat bogs

redshank, spotted redshank, green sandpiper, wood sandpiper, godwits, ruff

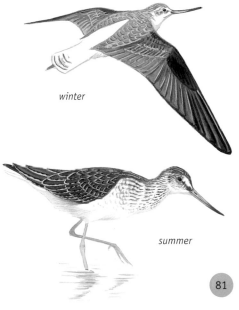

winter

summer

Green Sandpiper (21–24cm)

Keep a lookout in autumn, when this shy wader is most common.

- smaller and dumpier than Redshank, with straight bill and greenish legs; dark breast and upperparts contrast with white belly; **in flight, white rump and dark underwings**

- usually in ones or twos; stays near cover; picks for food; often bobs rear end; takes off with fast zig-zag flight when flushed, like Snipe

- *tweet, weet-weet* flight call

- passage migrant to inland waters in southern half of England, Wales and Ireland; a few overwinter; gravel pits, ditches and marshy lakeshores

- redshank, wood sandpiper, common sandpiper, ruff

Common Sandpiper (19–21cm)

This busy little wader rarely stops bobbing up and down.

- smaller than green sandpiper, with more crouching posture; brown head and upperparts; **brown breast contrasts sharply with white belly**; in flight, thin, white wing-bar but no white rump

- usually alone or in pairs; bobs up and down constantly; often perches on rocks; flies low over water with quick beats of down-curved wings

- shrill *swee-wee-wee-wee* flight call

- summer visitor to rivers and streams in hilly regions of north and west; passage visitor to lowland sites including gravel pits and sheltered coasts; some overwinter

- green sandpiper, wood sandpiper, dunlin

Ruff (20–30cm)

Look carefully: a 'puzzling' wader in autumn might well be a ruff.

summer

♂

♀

male is redshank-sized, female is smaller; small head and short bill; at most times, brownish-grey with **scaly pattern on back**; breeding male has colourful ruff of feathers around head and neck; in flight, thin, white wing-bar and white sides to rump

feeds singly or in small groups; picks at mud; lazy-looking flight; in spring, males gather to perform courtship displays (called leks)

mostly silent – except during courtship

passage visitor to lakes and coastal lagoons; rare breeding bird in East Anglia; some overwinter

green and wood sandpipers, redshank, greenshank

Snipe (25–27cm)

Camouflage markings make this secretive wader very hard to spot.

medium sized, with round body, short legs and **very long, straight bill**; complex pattern of stripes and bars

feeds alone or in small groups, seldom out in open; probes deeply into mud; flies off in fast zig-zag when flushed; in spring display flight, male vibrates outer tail feathers to make bleating sound (called 'drumming')

squaatch alarm call when flushed; 'drumming' sounds like sheep high overhead

widespread but not common breeding bird in bogs and marshes; more common in winter; prefers marshy ground at water's edge

green sandpiper, jack snipe, woodcock

FLEXIBLE FRIEND

A snipe's long bill looks as stiff and brittle as a twig. But the tip is actually sensitive and flexible, and can open under the mud. This helps the snipe to find hidden food such as worms and insect larvae.

83

Black-headed Gull (34–37cm)

This common small gull is often found far from the sea.

 smallish gull; bill and legs red in spring, white underparts, grey upperparts; head chocolate-brown in spring, otherwise white with dark smudges; in flight, **white stripe along front edge of wing**; young have ginger-brown markings

winter

usually moves in flocks; nests in colonies; 'paddles' with feet to stir up food; sits on water; catches insects in flight; follows ploughs

harsh *keyaar* call; very noisy at colonies

widespread inland or along coast; breeds on beaches and islands; common in winter on school playing fields and rubbish dumps

little gull, mediterranean gull, common gull, kittiwake (young)

summer

Common Gull (40–42cm)

Despite its name, this gull is less common than some others.

winter

summer

larger than black-headed gull; **greenish-yellow legs and bill** and dark eye; white head and underparts and grey upperparts; in winter, brown speckled head and neck; grey wings have black tips with white spots

usually in small numbers, often with black-headed gulls; may nest inland – or with other gulls; robs other birds for food

high-pitched mewing

breeds along the coast and in upland regions in Scotland, northern England and western Ireland; more common in winter; often on playing fields

little gull, black-headed gull, mediterranean gull, kittiwake (young)

Kittiwake (38–40cm)

Of all our gulls, the kittiwake is the only real 'sea' gull.

graceful, medium-sized gull; dark eye, small yellow bill and short, black legs; white head and underparts and grey upperparts; young have black 'W' pattern on wings; in flight, wings show two tones of grey; **neat, black wing-tips** have no white spots

breeds in big sea-cliff colonies – occasionally on dockside buildings; may follow fishing boats; never visits fields, parks or rubbish dumps

yowling calls at nest

breeds on steep sea-cliffs all around coast; spends winter far out at sea; rare inland

common gull, herring Gull, black-headed gull (young), fulmar

Herring Gull (55–67cm)

This noisy bird is a common sight in seaside towns.

large, with **fierce expression and heavy, yellow bill with red spot**; white, with grey back and wings; pink feet and yellow eyes; head flecked grey in winter; broad wings with white border and white spots on black tips; young are brown all over

nests in colonies on roofs and cliffs; joins mixed gull roosts; follows boats; raids bins in towns; sometimes aggressive; flocks fly high in formation

various loud mewing and wailing cries

common around coast all year and inland in winter

common gull, lesser and greater black-backed gulls (especially young)

RED MARKS THE SPoT

The red spot on a Herring Gull's bill is a target for its hungry chicks. When they peck this spot, the adult opens its bill and releases food into their mouths. The chicks' instinct is so strong that they will even peck the red spot on a plastic model.

Lesser Black-backed Gull (52–67cm)

This close relative of the herring gull often nests near its cousin.

- very similar in size and shape to Herring Gull, but with **yellow legs and slate-grey back and wings**; head flecked grey in winter; long wings narrower than herring gull's, with smaller white spots on black tips; young are brown all over

- nests in colonies; has wide diet and adapts to town life just like herring gull; joins mixed gull roosts

- mewing like herring gull, but deeper

- breeds around coast and on upland moors; widespread inland in winter; visits ploughed fields and rubbish dumps

- herring gull, great black-backed gull (especially young)

Great Black-backed Gull (64–78cm)

This powerful seabird is the king of gulls.

- biggest gull, with massive, yellow bill and stur pink legs; **blacker back and broader wings** th lesser black-backed gull; head flecked grey in winter; young are brown all over; in heavy flig can look almost like heron

- feeds like other large gulls, but hunts more live prey – including smaller seabirds; nests singly in colonies; joins mixed gull roosts

- gruff bark – *uk–uk-uk*

- breeds on rocky coasts and islands in north an west; also on large lakes; widespread inland in winter; visits ploughed fields and rubbish dump

- lesser black-backed gull (especially young), heron (in flight)

GULLS IN FLIGHT

Each gull has a different wing pattern, which helps you to identify it in flight. Remember that young gulls are much browner.

Lesser Black-backed Gull
(adult)
Herring Gull-sized; usually dark grey (not black) back.

Great Black-backed Gull
(adult)
Very big; very black above

Herring Gull (first winter)
Brown all over; looks like young black-backed gulls

Herring Gull *(adult)*
Grey back; black and white wing tips

Kittiwake *(adult)*
Silver-grey back; neat black wing tips with no white spots

Kittiwake
(first winter)
Bold black 'W' shape across back and wings

Common Gull *(adult)*
Similar to Herring Gull, but smaller

Common Gull
(first winter)
Brown and grey markings above; speckled head

Black-headed Gull *(first winter)*
Black and brown markings above; no black head

Black-headed Gull
(adult, breeding)
White flash down front of wings; fine black wing tips

Little Gull *(adult, non-breeding)*
No black wing tips; dark underwings

87

Common Tern (31–35cm)

This typical tern looks lighter and more delicate than any gull.

 smaller than black-headed gull, with longer, narrower wings and long, forked tail; white, with silver-grey upperparts and black cap; **pointed, red bill with black tip**; very short, red legs; darkish patch on primaries; white forehead in winter

light, bouncy flight, with head pointed down; sometimes hovers, before diving; never swims; often perches on posts; nests in colonies

high-pitched, grating *keee-yaaarr*

widespread summer visitor to coast and inland; uncommon in Wales and south-west England; nests on beaches and islands

arctic tern, roseate tern, black-headed gull, little gull

winter

summer

Arctic Tern (33–35cm)

This coastal bird migrates further than any other bird in the world.

AIR MILES

The arctic tern migrates further than any other bird. Each year, some fly all the way from their Arctic breeding grounds to their Antarctic wintering grounds and back again. An Arctic Tern that lives for 25 years may cover more than one million kilometres in its lifetime.

winter

summer

just like common tern, but with even lighter build, **longer tail and all-red bill**; soft, grey underparts make white cheeks stand out; dark line (not patch) along tips of primaries

flies like common tern, but more fluttery; often hovers in stages, before diving from quite low; nests in colonies

like common tern, but higher-pitched

summer visitor to northern and western coasts – especially Scottish islands; nests on islands and beaches; rare inland; spends winter at sea

common tern, roseate tern, black-headed gull, little gull

Sandwich Tern (36–41cm)

The earliest sandwich terns reach the UK coast late in February.

winter

summer

- largest tern, with shortest tail, heaviest bill and whitest plumage; black cap has shaggy crest in spring, white forehead in winter; **thick, black bill with yellow tip**; short, black legs; long, angular wings

- breeds in colonies, fishes in smaller groups; stronger and often higher flight than other terns; dives with splash (like small gannet)

- harsh *ki-rrrick*; noisy

- summer visitor to scattered breeding colonies around coast; nests on beaches and islands; widespread on passage; rare inland

- common tern, arctic tern, roseate tern, small gulls

Little Tern (22–24cm)

This dainty little tern is one of our smallest seabirds.

- smallest tern, with shortish, forked tail, large head and long bill; white, with grey back; **black cap has white forehead all year**; yellow bill has fine, black tip; very short, orange legs; narrow wings

- breeds in small colonies – usually in smaller numbers than other terns; flies with fast wingbeats; hovers and dives constantly

- shrill *krik–krik*

- uncommon summer visitor to scattered coastal breeding colonies – mostly in south-east and eastern England; nests on sandy and shingle beaches; rare inland

- common tern, arctic tern, black tern (winter)

winter

summer

Guillemot (38–41cm)

This upright seabird looks a little like a small penguin.

 woodpigeon-sized, with short tail, long neck and pointed bill; **white below, with chocolate brown head and upperparts**; some have white eye-ring; face and throat white in winter

breeds in dense sea-cliff colonies; perches on ledges, swims like a duck; dives from surface to catch fish; small wings look blurred in fast, low flight

growling calls at nest

breeds on steep sea-cliffs; most colonies in north and west, none in south-east; rest of the year at sea (usually in flocks), anywhere around coast

razorbill, puffin, black guillemot, sea ducks, divers (winter)

summer

winter

Razorbill (37–39cm)

You can often spot razorbills among large crowds of guillemots.

summer

winter

size and shape of guillemot, but with larger head and broad bill flattened like blade; **black upperparts** (guillemots are brown), with fine, white bar on wing, face and bill; face and throat white in winter

breeds on sea-cliffs; perches on ledges or swims like duck – with tail more cocked than guillemot; dives very deeply; fast, low flight

growling calls at nest

breeds on steep sea cliffs with guillemots; spends rest of year at sea, but less common inshore than Guillemot

guillemot, puffin, black guillemot, sea ducks

Puffin (26–29cm)

A colourful bill and comical expression make this a popular bird.

summer

winter

THE EEL DEAL

The small silver fish that puffins carry in their bills are called sand eels. They are the most important food for puffins and many other seabirds during the breeding season. When sand eels die out, so do puffins.

smaller than pigeon; **huge, colourful bill;** white below and black above; pale grey cheeks; clown markings around eye; red legs and feet; in winter, darker face and smaller bill

nests in colonies on grassy cliffs; perches near burrow or swims on sea, diving often; carries beakfuls of small fish to nest; fast, direct flight – like huge bumble bee

growling calls at nest

breeds on rocky coasts and islands; most common in north and west Scotland; also Wales, Ireland, north-east and south-west England; rest of the year at sea

razorbill, guillemot, black guillemot

Black Guillemot (30–32cm)

This auk is the least sociable and most northerly of its family.

smaller and plumper than guillemot; in summer, **black all over with oval white patch on wing;** in winter, white below and mottled grey above; bright red legs and feet; wing-patches always show in flight

usually in ones and twos; breeds in small colonies among boulders; swims like duck and dives deeply; fast, low flight, like guillemot

whistling *peeeee* at nest

rocky coast of north and west Scotland and Ireland (rare in England and Wales); spends winter on sea, close to breeding sites

guillemot, razorbill, puffin, small grebes (in winter)

summer

winter

Cuckoo (30–32 cm)

This unusual bird has a good reason for its secretive behaviour.

looks like small bird of prey, with pointed wings and long tail; grey upperparts, head and breast; white belly with black barring; rounded tail with white tip; thin, curved bill; young are brown, heavily barred

usually alone; lays eggs in other birds' nests (including dunnock, meadow pipit and reed warbler); often mobbed by other birds; flies low, with wings beating below body; calls in flight or perched; wings droop below tail when perched

loud *cuc-koo* in spring; female makes bubbling calls

widespread summer visitor; moorland, farmland, reedbeds and coasts

kestrel, sparrowhawk, pigeons

> ### A PERFECT MATCH
>
> *A cuckoo's eggs always match the colour of its host's eggs. For instance, an egg laid in a dunnock's nest is pale blue, while one laid in a reed warbler's nest is speckled brown. This way, the host never spots the extra egg – even though it's larger than its own.*

Feral Pigeon (31–34 cm)

This common city bird comes in many different plumages.

medium-sized pigeon; variable pattern of black, white, brown and grey – often with green or purple sheen on neck; **usually has white rump and black wing-bars**; wings white underneath

forms big flocks in towns; feeds on ground; roosts and nests on buildings; clatters wings on take-off; flies fast; glides and wheels with wings raised; very tame

bubbling and cooing calls during display

very common in many built-up areas; also cliffs, quarries and farmland.

collared dove, stock dove, woodpigeon

Woodpigeon (40–42cm)

Our biggest pigeon is also one of our most common birds.

bigger and plumper than feral pigeon; blue-grey body with pinkish breast and greenish-purple neck-sheen; white neck-patch (adults only); black tail band; in flight, **white crescent across middle of each wing**

sometimes alone, but forms big flocks during winter; feeds in trees and on ground; clatters wings on take-off; in spring display, male flies up from trees, claps wings above back, then glides down

rhythmic five-part cooing, *coo-ROO-roo, oo-roo*

very common in woods, parks and gardens; in winter, mostly on farmland

collared dove, stock dove, feral pigeon

Stock Dove (32–34cm)

This farmland bird is easily overlooked.

size and shape of feral pigeon; blue-grey body with greenish neck-sheen and pale rump; two short, black wing-bars near body, and black tail-band; dark eye; wings grey underneath in flight; **no white markings**

in pairs or small groups; often with Woodpigeons; feeds on ground; nests in tree holes; displays in circular glide with wings raised

soft two-part cooing, *ooo-woo, ooo-woo*

widespread, except northern Scotland and Northern Ireland; parkland and woodland edges with old trees; often feeds on farmland

collared dove, woodpigeon, feral pigeon

Turtle Dove (26–28cm)

The purring call of this summer visitor has become a rare sound.

 our smallest dove; slim, with diamond-shaped tail; blue-grey head, pink breast and **orange-brown back with black 'scales'**; black-and-white neck-patch; in flight, pale grey on wings and broad, white band across end of tail

in pairs or small groups, often in tree canopy; feeds on ground; in spring display, male flies up, claps wings, then glides down with tail fanned

cat-like purring, often from hidden perch

uncommon summer visitor, mostly to south and east England; open woods, parkland, and farmland with thick hedges

collared dove, feral pigeon

Collared Dove (31–33cm)

This common bird only started breeding in the UK in 1955.

slimmer and longer-tailed than feral pigeon; pale greyish-brown body; **thin, black bar either side of neck**; in flight, broad, white band at end of tail

often in pairs, seldom in flocks; feeds on ground; sings from roofs and wires; in spring display, flies steeply up, then glides down with wings fanned

loud, rhythmic, three-part cooing, *coo-COO-coo*

common everywhere except upland areas; likes gardens and farms, but avoids city centres; often visits bird tables

woodpigeon, feral pigeon, turtle dove

Barn Owl (33–35cm)

Look out at dusk for a ghostly white shape drifting over the fields.

smaller and slimmer than tawny owl; snow-white underparts; honey and soft grey upperparts; big head with heart-shaped face; long legs; long, rounded wings

usually alone; hunts mostly at dusk, sometimes also by day; flies slowly over fields in search of rodents; often hovers; nests in old farm buildings and sometimes on cliffs

eerie shrieks and hissing screams

widespread but uncommon; absent from parts of northern Scotland and western Ireland; rough farmland, woodland edges and coastal marshes; often near ditches and riverbanks

tawny owl, short-eared owl, gulls (in flight)

Tawny Owl (37–39cm)

Often heard, but seldom seen, this is the original 'brown owl'.

large, stocky (woodpigeon-sized) with big head; short, broad wings; **reddish-brown upperparts marked with white**; heavily streaked underparts; ring around face; white markings between dark eyes

usually alone; hunts at night and roosts in tree by day; swoops on rodents from perch; nests in holes; rarely seen by day unless flushed; often mobbed by small birds at roost; fast, silent flight

wavering hoot, *hoo-hoo-hoo*; female makes high shriek – *kee-wick*

widespread everywhere except Ireland; deciduous and coniferous woodland, parks, gardens and churchyards

barn owl, long-eared owl, short-eared owl

Little Owl (21–23cm)

This pocket predator is the smallest of our owls.

 very small (starling-sized), with large, square head and short tail; rounded wings. greyish-brown upperparts with white spots; heavily streaked underparts; fierce-looking, **yellow eyes with white eyebrows**

usually alone; hunts at night, but often seen by day; hunts small mammals and insects – also earthworms on ground; often perches on post out in open; nests in holes; undulating flight

high-pitched shriek – *kiew kiew kiew*

widespread in England, Wales and southern Scotland (not Ireland); farmland with woods, hedgerows and old trees

tawny owl

Short-eared Owl (37–39cm)

You might spot this owl out hunting by day.

slimmer and smaller-headed than tawny Owl; small 'ear' tufts hard to see; brown and streaky all over; yellow eyes with dark borders; in flight, **long wings pale below with dark bar at 'wrist'**

usually alone, but may roost in groups; hunts at dawn and dusk; flies low in search of prey; may glide like harrier; usually perches on ground or fence posts

low *hoo-hoo-hoo-hoo*, but usually silent

uncommon; breeds in northern and eastern England, Wales and Scotland; more widespread in winter; open country, including moorland and coastal marshes

barn owl, long-eared owl, harriers.

Green Woodpecker (31–33cm)

A loud call and a flash of green usually give this bird away.

♀

TIP oF THE ToNGUE

A woodpecker's amazing tongue is longer than its head and bill combined. It is rooted right at the back of the skull, and shoots out to capture small creatures hidden deep in holes. Tiny sticky barbs on the tip stop the prey from escaping.

♂

biggest woodpecker, with pointed bill and short, pointed tail; green above and greyish below; black face markings (with red in male) and red crown; in flight, **yellowish-green rump**

usually alone; on ground, digs for ants with bill; in trees, hops jerkily up trunk with tail pressed against bark and taps for food; nests in tree holes; bounding flight with bursts of flapping

loud, laughing *klu-klu-klu-klu* – often in flight

widespread except Ireland and north-west Scotland; open woodland and parkland; often feeds on lawns

great spotted woodpecker, mistle thrush, golden oriole (female)

Great Spotted Woodpecker (22–23cm)

This bark-basher often scatters other birds from the feeder.

song thrush-sized, with pointed bill and tail; black-and-white face and upperparts, with white oval on shoulder; cream below, with **red under tail**

usually alone; climbs tree trunk with tail pressed against bark; taps and probes for food; hangs from birdfeeders; may raid nestboxes for nestlings; bounding flight, with short bursts of flapping; seldom visits ground

loud *tchik!* call; in spring, drums bill against tree trunk in short, loud bursts

common anywhere with trees, except Ireland and northern Scotland; woods, parks and large gardens

lesser spotted woodpecker, green woodpecker

♂

Kingfisher (16–17cm)

A blur of blue may be all you see when a kingfisher flashes past.

 small (sparrow-sized), compact and upright; short tail and dagger-like bill; wings short and rounded; **orange below and greenish-blue above** (upperparts change colour with the light); white patches on face; pale blue back stands out in flight

shy; usually alone; perches quietly on overhanging branch; dives underwater to catch fish; sometimes hovers; flies fast and low; nests in riverbank tunnel

sharp, high-pitched *zeee*, or *zee-teee* in flight

widespread, except northern Scotland and western Ireland; slow-flowing rivers, lakes, canals in built-up areas; visits estuaries in winter

dipper (call and flight)

Swift (16–17cm)

This high speed daredevil hardly ever leaves the air.

AIR FLAIR

Swifts are true flying champions. They feed, mate and even sleep on the wing. Young swifts born in Europe fly to Africa and back at least twice before they are ready to breed. They may spend three years in flight without landing once.

larger than swallow, with small body and thin, curved wings; **crescent-shaped in flight**; blackish-brown with pale throat; looks paler in sunlight; short, forked tail; bill almost invisible

feeds in midair on tiny insects; flies very fast, with stiff, flickering wingbeats and long glides; in spring, noisy groups chase each other; gathers high up in flocks; only lands at nest site (usually on old, tall building); flies low before storms

harsh, screaming *screeeeee*; flying groups call together

common summer visitor everywhere except northern Scotland; often above towns and lakes

swallow, house martin, sand martin

Swallow (17–19cm)

Soon after leaving the nest, young Swallows set out for Africa.

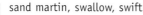 smaller than swift, with **long tail streamers** and more flexible wings; blue-black upperparts and breast band, white underparts and red face; in flight, white 'windows' in tail; young have shorter tail

feeds on insects in air; agile flight, but not as high as Swift; flies low over water and may touch surface; perches on wires, where flocks gather in autumn; nests in farm buildings

light *vit vit* call; long, twittering song

common summer visitor; farmland, villages, ponds; not city centres

swift, house martin, sand martin

House Martin (12.5cm)

This small relative of the Swallow shares its home with people.

smaller and more compact than swallow, with shorter, forked tail; blue-black upperparts and entirely white underparts; **white rump** in flight; young are browner

darting flight, like swallow's, but more fluttery and often higher up; perches on wires and roofs; small colonies nest under eaves of buildings; lands on ground to gather mud for nest

priit flight call; soft, twittering song

summer visitor everywhere except north-west Scotland; nests in towns and villages, but not city centres

sand martin, swallow, swift

99

Sand Martin (12cm)

This riverbank nester is one of our earliest summer visitors.

 slimmer than house martin, with less-forked tail; brown upperparts, and white underparts with **brown breast-band**; no white rump

flies like house martin; catches insects in air – mostly over water; perches on wires; small colonies dig nest holes in sandbanks; flocks roost in reedbeds

rattling twitter – harsher than House Martin

summer visitor everywhere except far north-west Scotland; more localised than house martin; feeds near nest sites – beside rivers or in quarries; flocks use reservoirs and reedbeds in autumn

house martin, swallow, swift

SPREADING SANDS

Fewer and fewer sand martins are visiting Europe. Their numbers may be falling because their winter quarters in Africa are shrinking. Farming and climate change is causing the Sahara Desert to expand, leaving many areas too dry for sand martins.

Skylark (18–19 cm)

You have to scan the skies to spot this springtime songster.

slightly larger than sparrow, with **short crest** (not always raised); brown above and pale below; streaked breast and upperparts; in flight, white outer tail feathers and white edge to back of rounded wings

feeds on ground; crouches when alarmed; flies up slowly to great height, then gradually descends, singing non-stop; forms large flocks in winter

liquid *chirrup* call; continuous, warbling song

common on farmland, grassland and upland areas; winter flocks in fields and along coast

woodlark, meadow pipit, tree pipit, buntings

Meadow Pipit (14.5 cm)

Up on the moors this is often the only small bird around.

Display flight

 smaller and more upright than skylark, with thinner bill and no crest; brown above and pale below; streaked back and breast; **white outer tail feathers**

 walks with wagging tail; often flutters around while calling; flies up in display flight (not nearly as high as skylark), then parachutes down

thin, whistled call, *see-see-see*; song is run of high notes accelerating to trill

common and widespread in open country and upland regions; winter flocks in fields and along coast – sometimes with Skylarks

tree pipit, rock pipit, skylark, woodlark

Rock Pipit (16.5–17 cm)

You might spot this pipit foraging among seaweed like a wader.

larger and darker than meadow pipit; brown above and pale below, with **smudgy, streaked underparts**; dark legs and bill; grey outer tail feathers

walks, hops and runs along shore; perches on prominent rocks; display flight like meadow pipit; often quite tame

single whistle, *pseep*; song like meadow pipit, but stronger

widespread on rocky coasts; uncommon in south-east England; feeds along shoreline and at base of cliffs; rare inland

meadow pipit, water pipit, skylark, shore lark

Pied Wagtail (18cm)

This busy insect-catcher is a common bird about town.

 sparrow-sized; **black and white with long tail**; black crown and bib; white face and belly; male has black back, female grey; young are browner, with brown breast-band

 usually feeds alone; walks and runs, wagging tail constantly; chases insects energetically; bounding flight; large roosts gather in town centres

🎵 sharp *chizik* flight call; simple, twittering song

🌍 common and widespread in open country, including towns; often (but not always) near water; likes roofs, lawns, car parks and school playgrounds

❓ grey wagtail, yellow wagtail (young), pipits (young)

Yellow Wagtail (17cm)

This summer visitor has a shorter tail than other wagtails.

🔖 shorter tail than pied wagtail; male **green above, with yellow face and underparts**; female duller; young has brownish 'necklace' on throat

🏃 runs like other wagtails, with constantly wagging tail; often feeds around feet of cattle; flutters after flying insects; small flocks gather on migration; bounding flight

🎵 loud *pseet* call, in flight or perched

🌍 summer visitor to England and southwest Scotland, but not Ireland; lowland farmland – especially marshes and water meadows; breeds near water; visits playing fields on migration

❓ grey wagtail, pied wagtail (young)

Grey Wagtail (18–19cm)

Look out for this wagtail beside water in the town or country.

♀

♂

summer

similar size to pied wagtail, with even longer tail; summer male is **yellow below, with grey back, black throat** and white eyebrow; female and winter male have pale throat and yellow only under tail

often in pairs; runs like other wagtails, with wagging tail; perches on rocks in water; bounding flight, low over water

sharp *tswik* flight call – shorter than pied wagtail

widespread; in summer, upland streams and rivers with weirs; in winter, lowland ponds, canals and even city roof tops

pied wagtail, yellow wagtail

Dipper (18cm)

This is the only bird that walks underwater along the riverbed.

plump body and cocked tail (like big Wren); adults **blackish-brown, with white bib** and chestnut belly; young grey above and pale below; short, rounded wings

usually alone or in pairs; perches on rocks in stream, then ducks underwater to feed; bobs constantly; takes off when disturbed; disappears around bend of river in low, buzzing flight; often nests under bridges

sharp *zit zit* flight call; soft, warbling song

upland regions, mostly in north and west; fast-flowing rivers or edges of upland lakes; follows rivers into towns during winter

wren, kingfisher (call and flight)

DIVING GEAR
The dipper is the only songbird that can feed completely underwater. It sees through transparent eyelids, and a special membrane of skin keeps its nostrils closed until it surfaces again.

Wren (9–10cm)

You might sometimes mistake this tiny little bird for a mouse.

 tiny, with cocked tail and sharp bill; very short, rounded wings; warm brown above, with fine barring and pale eyebrow; paler below

feeds alone; creeps about busily in roots, walls and low vegetation; in fast, buzzing flight looks like big bee; sings from raised perch; may roost huddled together

sharp, scolding *tik tik* call; loud, rattling song, usually ending in a trill

very common; almost every habitat – with or without trees; likes ivy and old walls

dipper (young), dunnock, goldcrest, mouse

SPARE NESTS

A male wren does his best to impress a female by building several nests. The female chooses just one in which to lay her eggs. If she has a second brood, she may use one of the spares. The rest are all abandoned.

Dunnock (14.5cm)

This quiet little bird usually keeps a low profile around the garden.

Wing-flicking display

sparrow-sized, with thinner bill; brown above, with black streaks; **blue-grey face and breast**; no eyebrow or pale markings

usually feeds alone; shuffles along close to ground, near cover; flicks wings; sings from prominent perch in bush or low tree; bullied by robins at bird table

piping *tseep* call; short, fast, warbling song

very common; almost everywhere except mountain-tops; likes mixed woodland, gardens, thickets and hedges

house sparrow (female), robin (young), wren

Stonechat (12.5cm)

This restless, noisy little bird usually makes itself very obvious.

summer

♂

♀

smaller than robin, with big, round head; summer male has **black head, white half-collar and orange breast**; female and winter male are duller; in flight, white rump and wing-patches

often in pairs; perches upright on top of low tree or bush, especially gorse; calls and flicks wings; drops down to feed

call, *hweet, chak-chak* – like stones struck together; warbling song like dunnock's

most common in north and west; moorland, heathland and coastal areas with gorse and heather; often on golf courses

wheatear, whinchat, redstart, robin

Wheatear (14.5–15.5cm)

A flash of white rump often reveals this early summer visitor.

 larger than robin, with upright shape and short tail; spring male is blue-grey above, pinkish-orange below, with black wings, black ear-coverts and white eyebrow; female and autumn male are browner; in flight, **bold white rump and white tail with black 'T-bar'**

feeds on ground alone or in pairs; runs after insects in short bursts; perches on rock or post; bobs up and down

hard *chak-chak*, like stonechat; warbling song

summer visitor, mostly to north and west; rocky moorland and upland pastures; coastal dunes and grassland; widespread on passage

whinchat, stonechat

♂

summer

♀

Robin (14cm)

This garden favourite can be less friendly than you might think.

- sparrow-sized, with upright stance, big head and thin bill; **orange-red breast and face** and brown upperparts, with blue-grey line between; whitish belly; young are mottled brown

- usually feeds alone; hops along ground or drops down from low perch (branch, post, spade handle); cocks tail; sings from high perch; rivals chase each other and fight

- urgent *tic tic* call; sweet, liquid, high-pitched song all year round, sometimes at night

- very common and widespread; woodland edges, hedgerows, parks and gardens; usually feeds near cover

- dunnock, redstart, black redstart, nightingale

> **SEEING RED**
>
> *Male robins fight fiercely over territory. The red breast of one acts as a trigger for its rival to attack. Young robins start life with a speckled brown breast. This keeps them safe from attack until they find a territory of their own.*

Redstart (14cm)

'Start' is an old word for tail, this bird's most striking feature.

♀

♂

summer

- slimmer than robin; spring male has blue-grey upperparts, black face and throat, white forehead and orange breast; female and autumn male are brownish above and pale orange below; young are mottled like young Robin; all have **orange-red tail and rump**

- flits through trees after insects; quivers tail; sings from high perch; seldom comes to the ground

- call, *hooeet* (like willow warbler); soft, warbly song

- Scotland, Wales and northern and western England (not Ireland); oak woodland and old pine forests; more widespread on migration

- black redstart, robin, nightingale

Black Redstart (14.5cm)

Look out for a flash of red tail on a city rooftop.

robin-sized; summer male is grey above and sooty-black below, **with white wing panels and an orange-red tail**; female, young and winter male are greyish brown with an orange-red tail

hops around buildings and rocks, constantly quivering tail; sings from rooftops; may hover after insects like flycatcher

warbling song, ending in strange crunching noise (like gravel path); short *tak, tak* call

uncommon; central and southern England and Wales; nests in city wasteland and industrial areas; winters on sea cliffs; widespread around the coast on migration

redstart, robin, house sparrow

Blackbird (24–25cm)

'Black' only describes the male of this common garden songster.

larger and longer-tailed than starling; male is **black with yellow bill**; female and young are dark brown with speckled throat and breast

feeds on ground; hops across lawn in bursts; stops to spot prey; rummages in leaf litter; tail jerks up when landing, then sinks slowly down; sings from prominent perch, such as bare tree or roof – sometimes at night; flies low into cover

many different calls, including shrill *chink chink chink*; rich, fluty song with many separate phrases

very common and widespread; woodland, parks and gardens

starling, ring ouzel, jackdaw

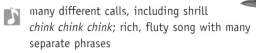

Song Thrush (23cm)

This garden bird is an expert snail smasher.

smaller than blackbird; unmarked brown face and upperparts; pale, **spotted underparts with orangish underwing in flight**; young have pale, streaked upperparts

often alone; feeds quietly on ground – usually near cover; hops in bursts, stopping to spot prey; smashes open snail shells by banging them on stone; direct, straight flight; sings from high, prominent perch

thin, *tsic* flight call; loud, tuneful song, with many phrases, each repeated up to five times

common and widespread; parks, gardens, woodland and hedgerows

female blackbird, mistle thrush, redwing, fieldfare, starling

FRUIT SUPPLY

Thrushes eat plenty of berries and other fruit. Try leaving out fallen fruit, such as apples, on the lawn. This can be a big help in hard winter weather, when other food is tricky to find. You may even attract redwings or fieldfares to your garden.

Redwing (21cm)

Redwings arrive in October to enjoy the autumn berries.

slightly smaller than song thrush; brown upperparts, **cream eyebrow and stripe below cheek**; pale, spotted underparts; reddish flanks; reddish underwing in flight

shy; flocks feed on berries or (later in the winter) on the ground; often with fieldfares and other thrushes; looks like starling in fast flight

soft *seeep* flight call, often heard overhead at night in autumn; jumbled song when breeding

common and widespread winter visitor to farmland, parks, hedgerows and orchards; rare breeding bird in north Scotland

song thrush, mistle thrush, fieldfare, starling, female blackbird

Mistle Thrush (27 cm)

This bold, upright bird is the largest of our thrushes.

bigger than blackbird and song thrush; greyish-brown upperparts; **whitish underparts with bold**, round spots; in flight, white tail-corners and pale rump

upright and obvious; often in pairs; feeds in open; strong, dipping flight (like woodpecker); may be aggressive towards other birds; sings from exposed perch, often in stormy conditions; early nester – high in tall tree

loud, rattling call; powerful, blackbird-like song, with separate repeated phrases

common and widespread; open woodland and parkland with tall trees

song thrush, fieldfare, female blackbird, green woodpecker.

Fieldfare (25.5 cm)

Each winter this handsome thrush visits the UK from Scandinavia.

slightly smaller than mistle thrush, with longer tail; reddish-brown back and wings, **grey head and rum**p, and thickly-spotted orangish breast; in flight, grey rump contrasts with black tail

sociable; flocks feed in bushes or on ground; feeds with other birds, including redwings, starlings and lapwings; loose flight – often high up; noisy flocks gather towards end of winter

chattering *chak, chak-chak* in flight; warbly song when breeding

common and widespread winter visitor; fields, parks, hedgerows and orchards; very rare breeding bird in north

mistle thrush, female blackbird

Sedge Warbler (13cm)

A glimpse of stripy face quickly identifies this reedbed songster.

slightly smaller than sparrow, with flattish head and fine bill; streaky brown above and pale below; dark crown and **bold, white eyebrow**; reddish-brown rump in flight

clambers among tangled vegetation, often near base; pops up to sing from bush; performs short song flight

scolding *chirr, chirr* call; long, chattering song, including sweet notes and chirrups; may mimic other birds' songs

widespread and common summer visitor; mainly damp habitats, including reed-beds, ditches and waterside scrub

reed warbler, marsh warbler (rare), wren

SINGING FOR SUCCESS

Like all birds, a male sedge warbler sings to attract a female. His complicated song contains thousands of different notes, including many stolen from other birds. No two songs are ever the same. He stops singing as soon as a female arrives.

Reed Warbler (13cm)

Even when singing loudly, this skulking warbler often stays hidden.

same size as sedge warbler, with longer bill and peaked head; **plain brown above** and pale below with white throat and faint eyebrow; reddish-brown rump in flight

climbs among reeds; often sings low down; builds nest on reed stems; favourite host for cuckoo

sharp *chrrr* alarm call; long, chattering song – more mechanical and less lively than sedge warbler

summer visitor to England, Wales and eastern Ireland; most common in south and east; reedbeds on lakes, marshes and ditches

sedge warbler, marsh warbler (rare)

Blackcap (13cm)

Berries provide winter food for this tuneful warbler.

♀

♂

size of great tit; male is brownish above and grey below, with **jet-black crown**; female and young are browner, with reddish-brown crown

feeds energetically in trees and bushes; eats fruit in autumn and visits bird tables in hard weather; sings from quite high up

harsh *tac*, and scolding *cherrr* calls; tuneful song, with rich, fluty phrases

widespread summer visitor, and all year in south; deciduous and mixed woodland, thickets, parks and large gardens

garden warbler (especially song), whitethroat, marsh tit, willow tit

Whitethroat (14cm)

This perky summer songster often pops up on top of a bush.

size of great tit, with longish tail and peaked crown; male has brown back, reddish-brown wings and grey head; **white throat** contrasts with off-white underparts; female is browner, but also with white throat

forages in thick vegetation; pops up to sing from top of bush; often cocks tail; jerky song flight in spring

scolding *tac, tac* and *cherrr* calls; short, scratchy song

widespread summer visitor, except Scottish Highlands; hedgerows, scrub (especially gorse, hawthorn and brambles)

lesser whitethroat, blackcap, garden warbler, dartford warbler

♀

♂

Willow Warbler (10.5–11.5cm)

This warbler's lilting song quickly tells it apart from the Chiffchaff.

- very small (size of blue tit), slim and neat; greenish-brown above and yellowish-white below; dark eye-stripe and pale eyebrow; pale legs

- forages busily among leaves in tree canopy; moves about while singing from exposed branch; joins mixed feeding parties in autumn

- soft, repeated *hoo-eet* call; sweet song starts softly and ends with flourish

- very common and widespread summer visitor; forest edges and clearings, young plantations, birch woods, parks

- chiffchaff, wood warbler

Chiffchaff (10–11cm)

This warbler's jerky song tells it apart from the Willow Warbler.

- just like willow warbler, with slightly rounder head and **dark (not pale) legs**

- forages like willow warbler, but more twitchy; moves about while singing from exposed branch; hovers to pick insects from leaf; joins mixed feeding parties

- *hweet* call, shorter than willow warbler's; bouncy two-note song – *chiff-chaff, chiff-chaff* – often repeated for a long time

- common and widespread summer visitor; woodland, parks and sometimes gardens; some overwinter in south

- willow warbler, wood warbler

Wood Warbler (12cm)

This is our yellowest warbler – usually seen high in the branches.

larger than willow warbler/chiffchaff, with shorter tail, longer wing-tips and bigger-chested shape; green above with yellow eyebrow; **yellow breast and white belly**; brown legs

forages high in tree canopy; very agile; flutters and hovers to catch insects; does not flick tail; performs fluttering display flight among trees

sorrowful *pew-pew* call; high-pitched, silvery song that ends in trill

localised summer visitor, mostly to north and west; rare in south and east; oak woods in upland regions; sometimes beech woods

willow warbler, chiffchaff

Goldcrest (9cm)

This tiny insect eater is the smallest bird in Europe.

tiny; short wings and needle-thin bill; greenish above and whitish below; **black-and-yellow stripe along crown** (orange centre not always visible); no eye-stripe; thin, white wing-bar; young has plain crown

always on the move; feeds high among branches, hovers beside leaves and may creep up trunk; joins mixed feeding parties; quite tame

very high-pitched *seee* call; weedling song – *tseedle-dee, tseedle-dee* – that speeds up into short trill

common and widespread; coniferous woodland, parks, gardens, churchyards with yew trees

firecrest, willow warbler, chiffchaff, wren

HARD TIMES

Winter can be tough for goldcrests. It's hard for these tiny birds to find food and survive the cold. More than a quarter of British goldcrests may die during one very cold winter. But, after several mild winters, the population quickly rises again.

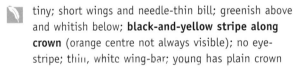

Spotted Flycatcher (14.5cm)

Look out for the aerial acrobatics of this expert insect catcher.

- sparrow-sized, with peaked head and longish wings; greyish-brown above and pale below, with **streaks on breast and crown**; young have pale spots on upperparts

- feeds by darting out from low perch to catch flying insects, often fluttering and hovering, then returning to same perch or another nearby; flicks wings while perched; often quite tame

- thin *zeee* call; soft, warbly song

- widespread but declining summer visitor; woodland glades, large parks and gardens with good mix of trees

- robin (young); redstart; pied flycatcher

Pied Flycatcher (13cm)

This black-and-white woodland bird sometimes uses nest boxes.

♀

summer

♂

- smaller and plumper than spotted flycatcher; summer male is white below and black above, with white forehead and **white wing-patches**; female and winter male are browner, but also with wing patches

- catches insects like spotted flycatcher, but does not return to the same perch; flicks wings and cocks tail; nests in tree holes and may use nestboxes

- sharp *huit* call; song a series of sweet notes

- summer visitor to western England, south-west Scotland and Wales; deciduous woodland – especially hilly oak woods; widespread on migration

- spotted flycatcher, great tit

Long-tailed Tit (14cm)

Over two-thirds of this bird's length consists of its tail.

tiny, with very long tail; pinkish below, black-and-pink back, thick black stripe either side of white crown; young has dark face

feeds in small groups, which flit one by one from tree to tree; acrobatic – often hangs upside down; roosts huddled together in cold weather; visits bird tables

high-pitched *see see* call, with short hissing trills – *tsrrrrr, tsrrrrr*

common and widespread, except far northern Scotland; deciduous and mixed woodland, hedgerows, parks and gardens with plenty of cover

pied wagtail, coal tit, bearded tit

Coal Tit (11.5cm)

This little tit often flees when bigger birds arrive at the feeder.

smaller than great tit, with big head; dirty white below and greyish-brown above; black head and throat, with white cheeks and white stripe down nape; two white wing-bars; young are greenish-yellow

usually alone or in pairs; feeds acrobatically and high up, may hover, or search trunk like Treecreeper; joins mixed feeding parties; stores food to eat later

thin *see see* call; loud two-part song, *pee-chew, pee-chew*

common and widespread; mixed and coniferous woodland, parks and gardens – especially with conifers

great tit, marsh tit, willow tit

Blue Tit (11.5cm)

This acrobat of the bird feeder is a regular garden visitor.

 smaller than great tit; blue-and-green above and yellow below (sometimes with thin, black belly-stripe); **white face with blue cap** and black line through eye; young are more greenish

feeds acrobatically on feeders and among outer branches, often hanging upside down; often dominates mixed feeding parties; nests in holes and nestboxes

thin *see see* call and churring alarm call, *see-see-see churrr*

very common and widespread; deciduous woodland (particularly oak), parks and gardens – including city centres

great tit, coal tit

CATERPILLAR COLLECTORS

A pair of blue tits collects hundreds of caterpillars each day to feed its growing brood. By the time the chicks have fledged, they may have gobbled up over 10,000 caterpillars. No wonder the exhausted parents look so tatty!

Great Tit (14cm)

Our biggest and boldest tit has many different songs.

larger (sparrow-sized) and sleeker than other tits; green above with blueish wings; yellow below with **thick, black belly-stripe** (wider in male); black head with white cheeks; young are more greenish-yellow

busy visitor to birdfeeders; often feeds on ground; may cling to tree trunk and tap bark; joins mixed feeding parties; nests in holes and nestboxes

churring alarm, and sharp chink call like Chaffinch; different songs, all with see-saw rhythm, *tea-cher, tea-cher, tea-cher*

very common and widespread; woodland, farmland, parks and gardens

blue tit, coal tit

116

Nuthatch (14cm)

Only the agile Nuthatch can climb down trees headfirst.

size of great tit, with short tail, big head and strong, pointed bill; rounded wings; blue-grey above and pinkish-orange below, with **bold black stripe though eye**

climbs busily up and down tree trunk and along high branches; taps loudly on bark, hammering nuts and digging out insects; visits feeders and feeds on ground; packs mud around entrance to nest hole; stores food

loud, repeated *dueet, dueet-dueet*; also *pee-pee-pee-pee* trill

widespread in England and Wales; rare in Scotland, none in Ireland; mixed and deciduous woodland, farmland, parks and large gardens

blue tit, great tit, treecreeper, woodpeckers

Treecreeper (12.5cm)

This quiet bird climbs quite differently from the noisy Nuthatch.

small and mousy, with pointed tail and **thin, down-curved bill**; streaky brown above with white eyebrow; clean white below; creamy wing-bars in flight

never still; shuffles up (never down) tree trunks like mouse, often spiralling round, then flies to base of next tree and starts again; probes for insects with bill; roosts in bark crevices; joins mixed feeding parties; doesn't use feeders

thin *tsee tsee* call; very high-pitched trilling song

common and widespread (except some Scottish islands); coniferous and deciduous woodland, parks and large gardens

nuthatch, wren, lesser spotted woodpecker

Jay (34–35cm)

A flash of white rump quickly gives away this colourful crow.

- pigeon-sized, with longish tail and short, thick bill; pinkish grey, with black moustache and pale crest on forehead; black-and-white wings with bright blue patch; in flight, shows **broad, white rump** and rounded wings

- hard to see; hops energetically on ground or through tree; buries acorns; raids birds' nests; visits birdtables and birdbaths; floppy, uneven flight – often one bird shortly behind another

- loud, grating screech (carries far through woods)

- widespread, except far northern Scotland and western Ireland; woodland (especially oak), parks and large gardens

- magpie, hoopoe (rare)

Magpie (44–46cm)

This bold, long-tailed garden visitor finds a meal almost anywhere.

NOT GUILTY!

Some people blame magpies for the decline of many garden birds. It's true that magpies eat eggs and nestlings. But studies show that they don't affect songbird populations. The real problem for songbirds is lack of food and nesting habitat.

- pigeon-sized; **black and white with strong bill and long tail**; black parts can shine green or blue; in flight, short, rounded wings show white patches on primaries

- alone or in groups; wide diet; walks or hops boldly on ground – often with tail cocked; perches on roofs; mobs cats and other birds; wobbly flight, with dragging tail; builds big nest in tall tree

- loud, rattling *shakashakashaka*

- common and widespread, except far north-west Scotland; woodland, farmland, towns, gardens, golf courses

- jay

Carrion Crow (45–47cm)

This intelligent and adaptable bird can live almost anywhere.

 bigger than magpie; completely black, with powerful bill; young are slightly browner; **black (not bare) base of bill**; in flight, square-ended tail

usually alone or in small groups, but may form flocks; walks or hops on ground; slow, steady flight; eats anything from worms to dead animals; builds big nest in tall tree

deep, cawing *kraaa, kraaa*

very common and widespread, except Ireland and western Scotland (where replaced by hooded crow); most rural and urban habitats – especially parks

rook, hooded crow, raven, jackdaw, chough

Hooded Crow: Very similar to Carrion Crow, but with pale grey back and belly; common in Ireland, and north and western Scotland.

Raven (64cm)

A deep croak often lets you know when a raven is about.

 biggest crow (bigger than buzzard); completely black, with massive bill and shaggy throat; in flight, diamond-shaped tail and longer neck than other crows

usually in pairs, but may gather in groups to feed; walks on the ground; in flight, soars like bird of prey and often performs tumbling aerobatics; eats anything from worms and eggs to rabbits and carrion; usually nests on cliffs

deep, hollow-sounding croak, *kronk, kronk*

cliffs, mountains and moorland, mostly in western regions; uncommon, but increasing

rook, carrion crow, hooded crow, chough, large birds of prey

Rook (44–46cm)

Gathering 'crows' in a farmer's field are most likely to be Rooks.

- slightly smaller than carrion crow, and shaggier, with peaked crown and 'baggy trousers'; glossy black, with purplish sheen; **pale bare patch at base of bill**; in flight, shows clearer 'fingers' than crow, and more rounded tail

- usually in large flocks; feeds in fields on grain and worms; often beside roads; nests in colonies (rookeries) at top of tall, bare trees

- grating croaks – *graarrr, graarr*; very noisy at rookery

- common and widespread, except north-west Scotland; farmland with woods; not city centres

- carrion crow, hooded crow, raven, jackdaw, chough

Jackdaw (33–34cm)

This neat, upright little crow finds a ready-made rooftop home.

- much smaller than rook, with stocky shape and short bill; blackish-grey, except for **paler grey hood and pale eye**; shorter, more rounded wings than rook

- usually in pairs or flocks; hops on ground or walks fast; gathers with rooks or starlings; dives and tumbles in flight (especially around cliffs); nests in holes – including chimneys; visits birdtables

- sharp *jack, jack*, and higher-pitched *kyow*

- common and widespread, except north-west Scotland; farmland, woodland, towns and villages; likes old buildings and sea-cliffs

- carrion crow, hooded crow, rook, chough, feral pigeon

Starling (21.5cm)

Waddling starlings squabble at the bird table.

winter

smaller and more upright than blackbird, with shorter tail and sharper bill; in summer, **oily-black with brownish wings and yellow bill**; speckled in winter; young are greyish-brown, with spotted belly in first winter; in flight, paler, triangular wings

feeds in groups; waddles on ground, probing with bill; waves wings while singing; may roost in thousands; visits feeders and birdbaths; fast, direct flight; huge flocks twist and turn in midair

complicated song with rattles and whistles; imitates anything – from other birds to telephones

common and widespread; power lines, lawns, rubbish dumps, seashore; may roost on bridges, piers or buildings

blackbird, jackdaw, waxwing (rare)

House Sparrow (14–15cm)

The decline of our best-known town bird has puzzled scientists.

small and plump, with short, thick bill; male is streaky chestnut above and pale grey below, with **grey crown and rump**, pale cheeks and black bib; female and young are streaky brown above with pale eyebrow

flocks around buildings; hops on ground; may chase insects in flight; colonies nest on roofs and roost in bushes; winter flocks gather on farmland; straight flight

simple chirps and chirrups

very common and widespread, though declining; always near human activity, such as farms and towns; not forests, mountains or moorland

tree sparrow, dunnock, chaffinch (female)

Chaffinch (14.5cm)

This neat finch is one of our three most common birds.

- slimmer than sparrow; pale, pointed bill; male has chestnut back, white wing-bars, **blue-grey head and pink breast and face**; female is more pinkish brown; in flight, white wing-bars, white outer tail feathers and greenish rump

- alone or in pairs; feeds on ground with nodding walk; sings from high perch; flocks with other finches in winter; bouncing flight

- loud *chink-chink* call; song is downward rattle ending in flourish

- very common and widespread; all habitats (often in places with few other birds); parks and gardens

- house sparrow (female), brambling

♂

♀

Goldfinch (12–13cm)

A flock of Goldfinches adds an extra splash of colour to autumn.

- small and agile, with longish bill; sandy brown, with black, white and red face; **black and yellow wings** very clear in flight; young have plain head

- feeds on low plants, such as thistles or dandelions; dangles acrobatically to reach seeds; nests in trees; gathers in large autumn flocks

- simple *twit-a-twit* flight call; long, twittering song – quite similar to swallow

- common and widespread, except in far north; likes rough, open country, such as wasteland, golf courses and road verges; visits garden feeders

- greenfinch, siskin, linnet

Greenfinch (15cm)

This chunky green-and-yellow finch is a confident visitor to feeders.

sparrow-sized; forked tail; male is mostly bright green; female is duller; **bold yellow markings on wings and tail** show when perched and in flight

feeds on seeds on ground and in trees; circular spring display flight from treetop perch, with slow wingbeats; joins mixed finch flocks in winter; likes feeders

during display, makes loud twittering trill followed by long, wheezy *dzeeeee*; also *chichichi* flight call

common and widespread; woods, gardens and farmland – also along coast during winter

siskin, goldfinch, yellowhammer, house sparrow (female)

Siskin (12cm)

This lively little finch often behaves more like a blue tit.

smaller than greenfinch, with narrower bill and nore forked tail; male is streaky green above, with **yellow breast and face, black cap and short black bib**; female is streakier with no black on face; bright yellow wing and tail markings

flocks feed acrobatically in treetops (especially alder and birch) – often with Redpolls; visits garden feeders in early spring

tzeuu or *tzuee* flight call; twittering, wheezing song

breeds mostly in coniferous forests – most common in north and west; widespread in winter in mixed woodland (often near water), parks and gardens

greenfinch, lesser redpoll, goldfinch

Linnet (13.5 cm)

This handsome songster is easiest to identify in spring.

slim finch, with small bill and forked tail; spring male has **chestnut back, grey head**, red forehead and red patches on breast; otherwise streaky brown, like female; in flight, white patch on primaries and tail

feeds on or near ground (never in trees), taking seeds from low plants; sings from top of bush; joins mixed finch flocks in winter

twittering flight call; twittering song, with scratchy and wheezy notes

♂

common and widespread except in far north; prefers rough open ground – especially with gorse; along coast in winter; seldom visits gardens

♀

chaffinch, redpoll, twite

Bullfinch (15–16 cm)

This colourful finch has a strong bill for plucking buds and seeds.

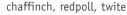

♀

plump, with thick neck and thick bill; male has rose-pink face and underparts, black crown, and grey back with pale wing-bar; female has same pattern, but browner and duller; young have plain crown; in flight, **broad white rump**

secretive and always near cover; feeds in pairs or small groups in trees or low plants; eats seeds and buds; doesn't flock with other finches

soft, sorrowful *pee-uu* call; quiet song

widespread, but declining; mixed woodland, farmland with hedgerows, orchards, parks and large gardens

♂

chaffinch, hawfinch, robin

Yellowhammer (16–16.5cm)

Look out for a yellow blob on top of a gorse bush.

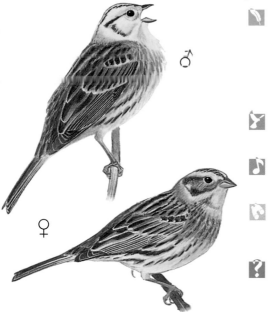

♂

♀

larger than sparrow, with longer tail; breeding male has streaky chestnut back, **yellow head** and streaky yellow breast; female and non-breeding male are duller brown with heavier streaking; in flight, chestnut rump and white outer tail feathers

feeds on ground; sings from top of bush; gathers in mixed winter flocks; dipping flight

grating *zit* call; short song all on one note except for last – *se-se-se-se-se-se-se-soo*

common and widespread; open country with hedgerows and bushes – especially gorse and hawthorn

cirl bunting (rare), corn bunting, reed bunting, skylark

Reed Bunting (15cm)

The male's bold black-and-white head stands out among reeds.

sparrow-sized; breeding male has pale underparts, streaky chestnut back and **black head with white collar and moustache**; female and non-breeding male are duller, but with well-marked face; in flight, white outer tail feathers

usually feeds close to water – often among reeds; male sings from bush; forms flocks in winter with finches and pipits

metallic *ching* call; simple song is a few repeated chirps

widespread except in uplands; mostly damp areas, including reedbeds, marshes and waterside scrub; also commons, farmland and young plantations

yellowhammer, house sparrow, tree sparrow, lapland bunting (rare)

♂

Wildlife Watching

Watching wildlife is fun. It can be exciting, it can be funny, and it is certainly fascinating. You can do it at home, at school, in your garden, from a car, train or bus. You can do it at any time of the year, and anywhere in the world. You can be a bit interested one day, and keen the next. You can spend hours and hours looking for wildlife, or just enjoy glimpses as you pass by doing something else.

Watching nature can also be useful. We need to know what's around us to know if any of it is in trouble and needs human help. And we also need to check that what we are doing to the natural world won't affect people too. But for now, just remember that nature watching is great fun and can inspire you for the rest of your life.

The first part of this section will help you to get the most out of nature. How to enjoy it. How to study it, what it is and what's worth looking for and when. It's all about helping you to become interested in wildlife.

The second part gives you a flavour of what to see in different habitats – woodlands, the seashore, and many more places.

The third part tells you a bit about the wildlife that you are likely to see, or that is worth seeking out for some special reason. It has some of the most famous wildlife, but also some that you may never have come across. There is so much to discover!

There is plenty in here, but there's also lots more than this to look for! I hope you like my selection and that it makes you keen to discover more.

Mark Boyd

What is wildlife?

Wildlife is any living creature, except human beings, that lives in the wild. So, a lion in the zoo isn't wild (even when it's rather cross), but a lion on the plains of Africa is wild, even when it's asleep. Pets and farm animals like dogs, hamsters, goldfish or sheep aren't wild. Their ancestors were wild, and they may do things in their own wild way, but we wouldn't call them wildlife.

What about the spider in your shed, or the weed in your flowerbed? These are still wild – they live their lives in places that suit them, but those just happen to be with us. They are as wild as your pet cat's fleas!

It's not always so easy. If gardeners grow a plant from abroad and it now grows where it likes, inside the garden and out, then it, too, has gone wild. And if people have brought plants or animals from abroad and let them go, either on purpose or by mistake, they will still seem wild. We call these non-natives, introductions or aliens – but they didn't come from outer space!

Sometimes what these non-natives do isn't welcome, from rabbits that eat a farmer's crops to rats and squirrels spreading diseases, but many are just colourful or interesting additions to our countryside, like golden pheasants and even apple trees. But wherever they first came from, they will all have their own fascinating stories for you to discover.

Nature is everywhere. In the countryside but also at home.

127

Being an active naturalist

You can enjoy the wildlife that you see day to day, or you can be an active naturalist. This means taking a special interest in the natural world, going places and doing things to increase your chances of seeing wildlife. And here's the thing. Active naturalists have more fun!

There are so many things to look for that many active naturalists do no more than learn the names of what they find. That's ok, but you don't have to stop there. Why not find out what wildlife you see does, what it eats and what eats it?

We know more about wildlife in the UK than anywhere else in the world, but every year new species are discovered. These might be windblown stray birds and insects that will never come back here again. However, some might be the start of a new wave of creatures that have moved in as our climate gets warmer or have been transported here with goods from other countries.

Every time you step outdoors, you can certainly find things that you have never seen before – you just have to choose to look.

Keep a record of your finds.

Starting out

Identifying wildlife sounds easy enough. It's just putting names to whatever you find. The trick is putting the same name to it that everyone else does! Identification is the starting point for all active naturalists. Once you know what something is called, you can find out more about it. You can then look it up in books or online and learn how what you find fits in with what else is known about the species.

For example, if you find an angle-shades moth on your wall in late November, you can look it up to see if that is a normal time of year to see the species. But first you have to know it's an angle-shades moth.

Is it a bird ... is it a plane tree?

The thing to remember when identifying wildlife is not to jump to conclusions and to use your common sense. Keep your options open. Only start to narrow your search down when you are sure you have picked the right group – you probably wouldn't confuse a bird and a tree, but is that minibeast you have found an insect, a kind of spider or a woodlouse? Get this right first or you'll start inventing all sorts of strange things.

It's best to decide on the group by looking at the creature or plant itself. Don't, for example, think that just because you saw a squirrel in the water, it's a watery creature – it may have fallen in!

Using a key

You can use a key to help, such as the one on the following two pages. A key is a process of questions and answers. So long as you get all the answers right, you can start to put a name to your creature. But be careful. One wrong answer and everything that follows it will also be wrong. So don't follow the key without thinking. After each answer ask yourself – does this still feel right?

Making your identification

Once you have decided which group your mystery wildlife falls into, you need to take it further – from animal to minibeast, to insect, to moth, to large moth, to angle-shades moth. The closer to making your identification you get, the more technical the language can become. Don't worry about that. It's only labelling that is there to help.

Keeping a record

Once you have taken your identification as far as you can on your own, it makes sense to record as much about it as you can. You can photograph it, write about it or draw what you have found. Drawing is often best because you can only draw something you have looked at properly.

Do this before looking it up, unless you can flick through a book with your mystery object still in view. Otherwise, when you start looking at the options you will start to doubt your own memory: how many legs did it really have? And what colour were they? If you have a record, you can look it up.

Checking your find

Now have a look in a suitable book that covers the wildlife in the area where you are looking (and preferably no wider). Were you correct about what you found?

A wildlife key

Answer each question truthfully and you can narrow down what you have found.
If you need more detail, invent more questions!

1 Is it a plant?

Probably green, not moving, maybe with flowers, twigs, seeds or nuts.

Yes   Go to 2.
No   Go to 7.

2 Is it a tree?

With a woody trunk or stem, branches, leaves, flowers or seeds, or surrounded by
fallen leaves in winter. Woody bushes count as trees.

Yes   Go to 3.
No   Go to 4.

3 Is it a conifer tree?

With thin, needle-like leaves, probably all year around, but perhaps bare in
winter with brown needles underneath on the ground.

Yes   Look up conifer trees on page 249.
No   Look up broad-leaved trees on page 250.

4 Is it a fern, moss, liverwort or seaweed?

Never with flowers, often in shaded, damp places, or washed up on the beach.
Probably green, red or brown.

Yes   Look up 'lower' plants on pages 260-261.
No   Go to 5.

**5 Does it look like a mushroom, with a cap and stem, or possibly growing out
of the side of a tree or rotting wood?**

Yes   Look up fungi on pages 262-264.
No   Probably a flowering plant. Go to 6.

**6 Does it have, or look like it should have flowers? Be careful, they may be
green, or tiny, or you may have found the plant outside its flowering season.**

Yes   Look up flowering plants from pages 251-259.
No   Try 1-6 again, or perhaps 15, if it was really an animal.

**7 Welcome to the world of animals. Let's start with the bigger ones. Did your
creature have feathers?**

Yes   It's a bird! Fly to page 56.
No   Go to 8.

8 Does it have four feet and fur?

Yes   It's a mammal. Run along to pages 188-203.
No   Go to 9.

9 Does it have no arms or legs, have fins and looks happiest underwater?

Yes   Go to 10.
No   Go to 11.

10 Does it have scaly skin and gills at the sides of its head?

Yes   It's a fish. Swim along to pages 208-211.
No   It's a whale, dolphin or seal – all mammals without feet! See pages 199-201.

11 Does it have scaly skin and live on land, or at least look as though it could walk with its legs (if it had any)? If you saw it swimming, did it keep its nose out of the water?

Yes   Sounds like a reptile. Go to 12.
No   Sounds like an amphibian. Go to 13.

12 Does it have four legs?

Yes   See the lizards on page 204-207.
No   Slither along to the snakes and slow-worm, page 204-207.

13 Does it have a tail?

Yes   Check out the newts on page 207.
No   Hop along to page 207 for the frogs and toads.

Not one of the above? You will be looking at an invertebrate – an animal without a backbone. Go to 14.

14 Does it have legs?

Yes   Go to 15.
No   Go to 16.

15 Does it have six or eight legs?

Yes   You have an insect or spider. Scamper along to pages 212-233.
No   If it has lots more legs than that, check out the centipedes and millipedes on page 242, and the crustaceans on pages 236-238.

16 Does it have an obvious shell?

Yes   Look up snails and shellfish on pages 240-241.
No   Sounds sluggy or wormy. See pages 245-246.

If you want to go further than this, make up some more questions. Just remember they have to be answered 'yes' or 'no' with no confusing 'maybes'.

Beyond counting

Observing wildlife doesn't have to be about numbers. Counting is important, but it's not the only fun you can have as an active naturalist.

You could choose to photograph, draw or paint what you see, or write down observations, stories or poems based on it. This is more personal because you are responding to wildlife, not just recording it.

Observation ideas

- Draw a tree from memory. Now go and look at a real tree and draw it from what you are really seeing. Try to move your pencil across the page at the same speed as your eye moves along each branch. You will probably have a better picture as a result. Even if you haven't you will have looked at that tree very actively.

- Find somewhere where there are lots of animals of the same type – a bird table, duck pond, deer park – and try drawing each one. When it moves, switch to another creature, but still draw from life. You will soon notice that each creature is different.

- If you haven't got a fancy camera, don't worry. Most phones have cameras that are good enough to take pictures of flowers, fungi and slow-moving insects.

- Bring all this together in a nature diary or blog. Fill it with counts of what you see, but also write what you felt about the encounter. In a year's time that description will bring the memory flooding back. Remember to include a note of the date, the weather and the location for every record.

Drawing tips

One way to draw is to look hard at what you see and try to simplify it into shapes such as circles, squares and triangles. Get those down in the right sizes and then adjust each shape to fit what you are looking at.

Another way is to imagine that there is a window pane between you and your wildlife. Now, draw what's on the window pane – this can help to make the 3D world flatter and easier to draw.

The naturalist's kit bag

All you really need to be a naturalist is a curious nature that gets you outside to see what we share our fantastic planet with. But you will get more out of it with a few key pieces of kit. You don't need all of this to get started, but try not to leave home without your essentials. It's best to keep some of these in your coat pockets rather than your backpack for easy access – and if you have binoculars, they should be out of their case and around your neck.

Essentials

- Notebook and pencil with lined and plain paper – write down or draw what you see and where. It will help to identify it later. Mark its cover with centimetres for use as a ruler. You can also use the white paper to reflect light onto a subject or isolate it from a background when taking its picture.

- Hand lens or bug box – you can look through the wrong end of binoculars close up as an emergency magnifier, but a proper one will be better. The type of bug box with a magnifying lid on lets you get a close view without an insect escaping.

- A couple of plastic bags – to use as a seat on damp ground, but mainly for collecting interesting things (although not live animals!). Freezer bags are strong, see-through, have useful twisted wire closures and a space to write on.

- Pooter – the perfect insect collector (see page 213 for how to make one).

- Camera – a phone camera may be enough, especially with a good zoom. You may choose to add a small tripod (such as a gorillapod).

Try to carry a few essentials, including notebook and pencil and a magnifying glass.

- Binoculars – beg, borrow or buy them, but binoculars aren't just for birdwatching. A good pair will fit your eyes well, focus closely enough to use for spotting insects and just make your wildlife watching so much better. Always try them before you buy.

- Collecting tubes – for picking up seeds, small insects or anything else that looks interesting.

- Small paint brush – for moving minibeasts without hurting them.

- Rubber gloves – to pick up anything you don't fancy touching with your hands.

- Field guides – or a smartphone full of apps – to identify what you see.

- String – 5m of strong string, for tying things together. You could also tie knots in it to measure larger objects.

- Cereal bar – emergency rations for hungry naturalists.

Other useful items

- Telescopic inspection mirror – for looking under things, such as ledges in rockpools, or under the caps of fungi without picking them; on top of things you can't reach or for reflecting light onto your subject.

- Torch – it's always useful to carry a small and powerful one with you.

- Tray or a pale umbrella – to catch insects in after you have beaten branches.

- Tweezers – for picking things apart, such as pellets, or picking up tiny objects like seeds.

- Sticky tape – for attaching hairs, seeds or other finds to a page of your notebook – though not live animals!

- Small paper envelopes – for collecting seeds.

- Polarising sunglasses – for reducing reflections when watching fish and rock-pooling.

- Sun cream – especially for the back of your neck if you are spending time on your hands and knees looking at ground life.

- Pocket microscope – if you want to look at the world in detail.

- Bat detector – for bats, but also good for grasshoppers and crickets.

- Plastic spoon – for singling out pond creatures in a collecting tray.

- Sandwich box – for sandwiches, of course, but good protection for anything delicate you collect.

- Pencils – take two sharpened ones and you probably won't need a sharpener with you. Using crayons is one of the quickest ways of drawing things you can't bring home.

- Watercolour kit – a small, lightweight kit with just a few colours. One small brush will be enough.

- Water bottle (with water) – not just to drink or for your watercolours, but a bit of water can soften a dragonfly skin to make its joints move again, can encourage a sleeping slug or snail to reveal itself and can make the colours of pebbles come alive.

- OS map – to show where the best wildlife features are likely to be.

- Smartphone – for emergencies, reference and apps and maps.

- Seed for tame birds – you'll get a better look at ducks if they come close to feed.

- Sweep net – for butterflies, but also for sweeping beetles and spiders out of long grass.

A sweep net can catch flying insects as well as those sitting on wildflowers.

The naturalist's bedroom

You don't have to stop watching wildlife just because you have come home, so see how much of this you can get into your home biology lab. Your parents may call it your bedroom, but you'll soon have other ideas!

- Computer and scanner
- Nature table
- Microscope
- Collapsible insect-rearing cages
- Television
- Plants growing and drying
- Telescope
- Tripod
- Bookshelf full of field guides
- Old fish tank for temporarily housing creatures that you want to have a closer look at. Try to make it feel like the wild, with a bit of soil, a few plants and perhaps a water dish.

A microscope and scanner are useful to have around.

The naturalist's wardrobe

There's no naturalist style guide, but it's good to have a few of these in your wardrobe:

- Hat with a peak   to shade the sky, stop twigs poking your eyes at night and to keep the rain and sun off.

- Footwear to cope with a range of terrain.

- Coat with pockets so you don't have to carry a bag everywhere.

- Quiet, warm, rustle-free clothing in dark colours.

- You don't need to wear full camouflage unless you want to hide from other wildlife watchers!

- And remember to have something bright to put on if you are crossing roads at night. Remaining hidden from deer and badgers at night is fun. Remaining hidden from drivers is dangerous.

Dark clothing will make it less likely that wildlife will see you.

The naturalist's year

Spring

Spring starts in the warmer south and west and slowly moves north and east at around 0.5-1 mph across the 600 miles from Land's End to John O'Groats. This means that March is a spring month in south-west England, but April is still a winter month in much of Scotland. Spring won't reach the far north until May.

In any one place, though, spring is usually our briefest season. It is marked by the first flush of catkins on the trees, primroses and bluebells in the woods, the arrival of thousands of nesting seabirds on cliffs and islands, butterflies along country lanes and birds singing from every bush and tree.

It is a time of growth, arrivals and departures, and naturalists like to get out and note when all the different events of spring take place. When did you see the first swallow last year? When did you see your first flowering primrose the year before that? Can't remember? Well, spring is the perfect time to start a wildlife diary so that you never forget again.

These dates are so important that a whole science has grown around them. It is called phenology, which is the study of timing in nature. If you keep a spring journal or wildlife diary from now onwards, you will be surprised at how much these dates will change. In the past 40 years, spring has come earlier for plants by around 10 days, for birds by about a week and for insects by about two weeks. Who knows what will happen in the next 40 years?

Watch for frogs heading to ponds to breed.

Look for:

- Singing birds.

- Wildflowers in woodlands and then in the hedgerows.

- The first baby rabbits, foxes and badgers above ground.

- Brimstone, orange-tip and peacock butterflies.

- Frogs, toads and newts heading to the ponds to breed.

- Leaves opening on trees.

- Freshwater fish warming themselves up in the shallows.

Summer is a great time to watch wildlife. The days are long and warm. This not only gives you plenty of time for looking, but also means that some of the night creatures have to venture out in daylight to find enough food.

A lot of wildlife, from flowers to dragonflies, can only be seen in the summer months. And even then, some things only come out when it's sunny. For example, don't bother looking for most blue butterflies unless the summer sun is shining.

Reptiles, amphibians, bats and dormice will be active, if still hard to see. And thousands of migrant birds will be taking advantage of the long feeding days to nest here.

In later summer, many of the birds will hide away to replace their worn-out feathers in private. Many birdwatchers then turn their attentions to other wildlife – orchids, moths, butterflies, dragonflies, hoverflies or bats, for example.

We tend to think of the summer as being at least June, July and August, but some big autumn events may happen in those months. By mid-July most seabirds will have left their nesting cliffs, cuckoos will have gone and by the end of August all of our swifts will already have left for Africa.

Most wildflowers have finished blooming before the end of June, and some hedgerow fruits are ripe before the end of August. Perhaps we are better off not thinking too much about what we call the season!

Look for:

- Seabirds on their cliffs.

- Dragonflies and damselflies on every pond, lake and river.

- Listen for the squeaky calls of baby birds and watch them being fed by their parents.

- Caterpillars under nettle leaves and on ragwort plants.

- Bats on warm summer evenings.

Look out for puffins on cliffs.

Autumn

When does summer turn into autumn? Sooner than you think, and certainly sooner for some wildlife than for others. If waders have failed to breed in the High Arctic, some may start south on their 'autumn migration' as early as late June. Then again, in mild years, some trees may still have leaves as late as December. In other words, autumn is a season determined by what is happening in nature itself, rather than the date on a human calendar.

Autumn is a time to prepare for the hard winter to come, but it is also the time to cash in on all the summer growth. At the same time as there are more young birds and animals around that need food, there are also more seeds and fruits (and young animals) for them to eat. This means that as the temperatures start to fall and the nights start to draw in, the natural world becomes an even more exciting place for a naturalist.

Autumn is horse chestnut time.

Look for:

- Fruits, nuts and seeds in woods and hedgerows.

- Squirrels and jays collecting acorns for the winter.

- Swallows and martins gathering on wires before migrating south.

- More toadstools in any habitat.

- Special moths with fantastic names that only come out in autumn, such as the rosy rustic or merveille du jour.

- Groups of birdwatchers all peering intently – it is the season of rare migrant birds and their dedicated followers!

Whether it's damp, grey and miserable, bright and frosty, or icy and snowy, winter has two characteristics that affect your life as a naturalist and wildlife's fight for survival: it is cold and the days are short.

However cold we may think it is, winters in the UK are warmer than in much of mainland Europe, so we are the winter destination of choice for thousands of birds: whooper and Bewick's swans, pink-footed, brent and barnacle geese and thousands of ducks and wading birds head for our coasts and wetlands to spend the winter.

Smaller birds, especially tits, starlings, finches and buntings, flock together in winter to feed as well. So winter is a great time to see lots of birds.

Look for:

- Deciduous woodlands – the shapes of bare trees without leaves can be easier to see.

- Animal tracks.

- Nests, squirrel dreys and witches' brooms (a disease) in bare trees.

- Occasional moths.

- Fungi.

Bullfinches are quite shy, so it is easier to see them in a tree without leaves.

School holidays

Birdwatchers can get a bit frustrated that the most exciting and unpredictable times – the spring migration, the breeding season and the autumn migration – all mainly happen during the school term. You can still see plenty of birds in the school holidays, but if your interests are wider than that, you can fit lots of wildlife watching into your holidays.

Summer holiday: the best time for butterflies and moths, dragonflies, upland flowers, reptiles.

Autumn half term: look for wildfowl migrating and geese streaming into our wetlands. Search the woodlands, sand dunes, hedgerows and heathlands for fungi. Look for hedgerow trees full of fruit, and keep an eye on them over the winter to see which birds and mammals are scoffing the lot!

Christmas holidays: fieldfares and redwings will be all over the fields, and a light sprinkling of snow is great for showing up animal tracks. Some of our trees are easy to identify without their summer leaves. Identify and remember what they are in winter – as they will be the same species in the same place in the summer!

February half term: in southern England, you may see the first signs of spring. Wherever you live, now is the time to start learning birdsong, because there won't be many species singing. Get to know them now and you will be ready to learn the new arrivals later in the spring.

Easter holidays: often the best time for early flowers, migrant birds, the first butterflies, baby rabbits.

Spring half term: if you are not stuck indoors revising for exams, spend the whole of this week out watching nature! It's the best time, with bluebells, badger cubs, the magnificent dawn chorus of bird song, newts in the ponds and all sorts of life bursting from every tree and bush. Get out there now!

Get out to see the bluebells in spring half term.

Wildlife obviously exists all the time, but you will have your best chance of seeing it if you know when it is most active. In general, dawn and dusk are the best times, but not for everything. Butterflies and dragonflies need the warmth of the sun to be really active, and some flowers only open in the middle of the day.

Even most of the animals we think of as nocturnal come out at dusk. Tawny owls and some bats wait until it is really dark, but even so you can sometimes surprise them at the other end of the night.

In the spring and summer, most birds will be active from dawn for a few hours. They may stop moving about altogether by around 10am, so prepare for early starts. At least once in June or early in your summer holidays, try to get up and out before dawn – you will be amazed at how different the world of wildlife is before most people get up.

Some creatures, such as snakes and lizards, need to warm up before they can move about and feed. You can sometimes see them basking in early morning sunshine. Later in the day, they will move too fast to spot.

Most moths and a lot of other insects come out only at night, but not all of them. There are more day-flying moths than butterflies in the UK.

Remember that some habitats become much more dangerous after dark, such as woodlands where twigs can poke at your eyes, or the coast where the tide can creep up behind you. Be careful. You need to be watching at the best time for wildlife watchers as well as for the wildlife itself.

A grass snake takes an early morning sunbathe.

Weather watch

Without rain and all the other different sorts of weather we get in the UK, we wouldn't have such a wide range of wildlife to enjoy. Here are some tips about what to look for in different kinds of weather.

Rain

Look for slugs, snails, frogs and toads on the wet ground, and watch for pigeons and jackdaws lifting their wings on rooftops to wash their wing-pits! Don't look for ducks, bats or butterflies because they will either be sheltering or not looking their best.

Snails are attracted to the wet ground.

Cloudy days

Birds are often more active for longer on cloudy mornings, and they are easier to see high in the trees than against a bright blue sky. The lack of deep shadows can also help when trying to spot deer under trees. Some pale flowers look better out of the sunshine.

Colours of flowers or flying birds may look very different on a cloudy day.

Snow

Look for animal tracks after snow, but also look for newly arrived birds that have come in to avoid bad weather. In the right places, with the right luck, you may spot a white mountain hare or even a white stoat.

Look out for bird tracks in the snow.

Bright sunshine

Butterflies, dragonflies and other insects will only be really active in sunny weather. Sunlight shining into water helps you spot fish below the surface. Don't forget that some flowers open only in the sunshine.

Wind

Birdwatchers pray for onshore winds, especially autumn winds from the east. These will bring birds closer to shore to be seen and migrant birds and insects will blow in from Europe and Asia. Strong westerly winds blowing right across the Atlantic Ocean can even bring rare birds and butterflies here from America. That's 2,000 miles over the ocean, without landing once. Other wildlife may avoid the wind, but it can help you get closer to some animals if the wind is blowing your human scent away.

Fog

You may not be able to see much in fog, but when you do, you can often get quite close to it. Sound can travel well in fog and mist, but wildlife can often look much bigger in the gloom. Don't be fooled into thinking that Tibbles the cat is a mystery black panther!

Sound travels well on a foggy day like this.

145

Site guide

You can find wildlife anywhere, but there are real hot spots, with special creatures, huge numbers or easy viewing. Many are nature reserves, looked after for wildlife and wildlife watchers alike, but some are simply stunning places to be. Visit as many as you can. In general, head north and west for big numbers, and south and east for more variety.

Top places for:

- Marine nature reserves – Lundy Island (1), St Abbs Head (2), Kimmeridge Bay (3)
- Seabird colonies – Bass Rock (4), Farne Islands (5), Skomer (6), Rathlin Island (7), Isles of Scilly (8)
- Mountain and moorlands wildlife – the Cairngorms (9)
- Wildflowers – Malham Tarn (10), Old Winchester Hill (11), The Outer Hebrides (12)
- Red kites, as well as lots of other wildlife – Gigrin Farm (13), Welsh oak woodlands (14)
- Fantastic wetlands – Titchwell (15), Wicken Fen (16), Leighton Moss (17), Minsmere (18)
- Great wildlife spots – New Forest (19), North Norfolk (20), Minsmere (18), Wicken Fen (16), Isles of Scilly (8), Shetland (27)
- Wader flocks – Snettisham (21), Morecambe Bay (22)
- White-tailed eagles, divers, otters – Isle of Mull (23)
- Wildfowl – Slimbridge (24), Caerlaverock (25), Welney (26)

Thousands of wading birds live on Morecambe Bay.

Patch work

The UK has lots of wildlife because our land is so varied and is used in so many different ways: including farmland for crops and animals, woodlands, mountains, lakes and rivers, the coast, heathlands and many more. As a wildlife watcher, you can only ever hope to get to know a small part of it really well. And if you want to compare wildlife between seasons and years, you will need to focus on somewhere that you can go regularly and learn about – we call this area your 'local patch'.

What does a good local patch need?

- Easy regular access in all weathers.

- Water – whether it's a canal, river, reservoir or a sea bay, you find more wildlife near water.

- Trees – the more different types and the older the better.

- Not too many people, especially dog-walkers. You won't see much wildlife if dogs scare it away.

- Good places to watch from.

- Somewhere you like going – although once you start spotting wildlife you will like it anyway!

- Open, sunny areas, such as a south-facing grassy bank, where flowers will grow and insects will warm themselves up.

- A good route around it.

- To be safe – watching wildlife is exciting enough without putting yourself in danger.

Get to know your local patch by going there regularly.

Finding your patch

Ordnance Survey maps and Google satellite maps are a great way to start looking for your perfect local patch. See if you can work out a route that takes you through several different habitats. You may need to ask permission to go to some places, and you will need to let your parent or guardian know where you are going, but there is nothing like having a regular circuit that you know well.

Even if you live in the middle of a city, there will be places you can go.

Local canals and waterways can often be used as your patch.

Making tracks

The term 'tracks' can mean two things. It's the path a creature takes when it is going about its daily business, or the foot, beak, tail or other prints it leaves behind. A common way to find the path an animal takes is by seeing where it leaves its footprints. But be aware, many animals don't take fixed routes, so they will leave footprint tracks all over the place.

Rabbits, badgers and deer all tread pathways so regularly that they form tracks. Even without footprints, you can often tell what creature made them. Badgers, for example, almost always go under obstacles in their way. Deer and rabbits jump over them. So if you see a woodland path that goes under a fallen branch without any plants growing through it, you have probably found a badger track.

Some animals leave a trail that you can smell. Foxes and grass snakes both leave strong, sharp smells that are rarely forgotten. And sometimes you will find the animal at the end of its track – a slug on its silvery trail or the winkle creeping across the bottom of a sandy rockpool.

When you find a footprint, count its toes. Are there claw marks or foot pads? Is there a line where a tail has been dragged through behind the feet? Tracks can tell you what the creature was doing. Tracks made by a running animal will not only be deeper but differently spaced from those made while just ambling about.

Tracks can also tell you how long ago an animal passed through a place, or whether a hole is being lived in. Sprinkle a bit of damp sand in front of a hole and come back the next day to see if there are new tracks in it. If so, someone's at home.

Track tips

- Count the number of toes, claws and webs on tracks you find. Badgers have five toes with long claws, for example, and some birds don't have a rear claw.

- Look for different shapes of front and back foot tracks.

- Look along the lower strand of barbed wire fences, for animal hair. Badger hair has three colour bands; fox hair is red, and deer hair is hollow and stiff.

- Look at any bunches of feathers you find. If a fox catches a bird, it will bite through the feathers; if a sparrowhawk is the killer, it will pluck the feathers so they will be whole.

- Look under any leaves with holes in. You may find a happy vegetarian.

Poo and other waste

Animal poo and bird sick may not sound lovely, but they are useful for wildlife watchers. They can tell you what wildlife is in the area, how many there are, where to find them and what they have been eating.

If you find animal poo, it means the animal in question was there not too long ago. If you hadn't thought of looking for it there, that will be helpful. Some animals always poo in the same place, so that will tell you exactly where to find them. Badgers have family toilets called latrines, and woodpigeons and other birds may sleep and poo in the same place for several nights in a row, so if you find a pile, step aside and look up!

Some animals send messages with their poo: this is my place! So if you find it somewhere very obvious, such as on a river bank stone, it's an animal staking a claim. Very smelly poo may contain chemical signals to rivals or potential mates.

Pellets

Many hunting birds sick up pellets of fur, bones, insect shells and other indigestible material. Owl pellets are the most well known, but kestrels, herons, and even crows will produce pellets too.

Taking pellets apart is a great way not only to find what an owl has been eating but also to discover what small creatures are found in the area. Skulls of mice, voles, shrews and small birds remain whole in pellets and are easy to identify. Soak the pellet in a bit of disinfectant and you can then tease it apart with cocktail sticks or tweezers to see what was on the menu!

Poo facts

- If it has white in it you have probably found bird poo.

- Small piles of poo are usually left by plant eaters such as rabbits and deer.

- Bat poo in roofs dries out and is completely harmless and not smelly. It can even help insulate the roof.

- Insect poo is called frass.

- Predators have the smelliest poo!

Why not make a skull collection from pellets?

151

Holes and homes

Most animals don't think of homes in the way that we do, as bases from which to explore our world and return to for safety. Some do, such as badgers, rabbits, some spiders, crabs and even snakes. But more often, creatures only use them for one purpose – raising a family or sleeping – and they may move around a lot. Other creatures don't build a 'home', but return to the same place to rest, like limpets which return to the same piece of rock at low tide after spending the high tide under water eating algae.

Classic holes

- Mining and mason bee holes: less than 1cm across, and dug into sandy soil or soft walls, usually south-facing.

- Razor shell holes: a small hole low down on a sandy beach just above the sea may have a 25cm razor shell living in it.

- Vole holes: 2-3cm holes in grass may lead into vole tunnels.

- Rabbit holes: up to around 15cm in diameter and usually built into a hedgebank or woodland edge, perhaps under a bramble bush – there are likely to be several together.

- Fox earth: a single hole that is usually taller than it is wide, perhaps 15x25cm or bigger. Dug deeper into the ground than a rabbit burrow, so with a bigger spoil heap. Often with scraps of bone or other food around. Can smell sharp.

A fox cub by its earth.

- Badger sett: a group of large holes, wider than tall, each with a large spoil heap and possibly straw bedding by the entrance. Paths connect these holes to outlying ones.

- Kingfisher and sand martin holes: dug into soft river banks or sandy quarryside. Martins nest together in colonies.

- Brown hare's form: slight dips in the ground on a field track may be where a brown hare sleeps for the day.

- Squirrel's drey: a large untidy bundle of leaves and twigs high up in a tree.

- Harvest mouse's nest: a tightly woven ball of grass about the size of a tennis ball in rough grass or attached to reeds.

- Magpie's nest: a big single ball-shaped nest of twigs high in a tree.

- Rookery: where rooks breed together in groups. Lots of big untidy nests together high in trees.

A squirrel's drey.

A kingfisher enters its nest hole.

Bringing wildlife to you

Wildlife has simple needs – food, water, the right climate, somewhere safe from predators and safe to raise a family. Together, we call these things a 'niche'.

Every plant or animal has a slightly different niche, but many overlap. You may find plantains and dandelions growing on a grass verge, for example, but the plantains will be on or right next to the footpath because they are better at coping with being trodden on. They have tougher leaves that spread out close to the ground. We call this adaptation. Every plant or animal is adapted to live in its own niche.

Using niches

When you start to recognise the different niches, you can start to work them to your advantage. Birds need food and somewhere to nest, so by feeding them and putting nestboxes up somewhere where you can observe them in secret (such as your garden) you will bring them in.

Many wildflowers need poor soil and don't like mowing, so by leaving part of a lawn uncut and unfed, you may find wildflowers start to grow – and you can always add seeds. And once you have your wildflowers, you will start seeing more insects coming to feed on them.

Bumblebees and mining bees may need nest holes, hedgehogs may want somewhere to spend the winter, and pond life will need a pond!

Wildflowers will attract insects.

Tips for attracting wildlife

- Try making squeakilly noises by kissing the back of your hand loudly. This can bring small birds out of bushes (birdwatchers call this technique 'pishing').

- Squeak loudly through pursed lips to a barn owl and it may come to investigate you.

- Hoot at tawny or little owls and they may hoot back – and sometimes come to frighten you away, so be careful.

- Squeak at weasels, stoats and mink and they come to investigate because it probably sounds like an injured animal – an easy meal.

- Squeak at rabbits and they will run away – they don't want to be near what sounds like an easy meal!

- Push twigs or small branches into the mud at the edges of ponds for dragonflies to perch on – it can work for kingfishers, too.

- Leave a bathroom light on and its window open on summer evenings to attract moths and lacewings in (it's easier to catch a moth in a bathroom than in the clutter of your bedroom).

- In March, knock on the base of a big tree in a wood with a stick. A woodpecker may come to have a look at you.

- Make your own window hide – cover part of a window but leave eye holes. Then put a bird feeder just outside so you can have a good look.

- Make your own garden hide – an old sheet or netting over a garden chair will do – just so you can see out and wildlife doesn't think you look like a human.

- In dry places, provide water for drinking and bathing.

- Make a pond – the bigger the better.

Build a pond and wildlife will find it before long!

Wildlife gardening

If we could put all our gardens together, they would be bigger than the combined area of our national nature reserves. So if we could make them all better for wildlife that would be brilliant. Most gardens are a bit like the edges of woodlands, so it's not surprising that a lot of garden wildlife also lives in woods. That's obvious for birds, hedgehogs and butterflies, but it also goes for many other insects.

The more countryside features we can include in our gardens the better they are for wildlife, and the more of it you will be able to see, however big or small your garden. Even a city window box will attract bees and hoverflies.

If bats pass through your garden, they may like a bat box.

- Make a wildlife pond – even a small, temporary pond will fill with wildlife. If you can make a permanent pond, make it at least 50cm deep to stop it freezing solid in winter. Plant it with native pond plants (garden centres should know which ones will be suitable), and don't put fish in it.

- Make a compost heap – it will fill up with insects, centipedes, worms and snails, and if you are really lucky, a hedgehog or grass snake may choose to nest in it.

- Make a log pile – take logs of at least 10cm diameter and stack them up in the corner of your garden – it will soon be colonised by spiders, beetles and woodlice among other things. That will then attract wrens.

- Place a few flat sheets of metal, plastic or roofing felt down and leave them in place. Check underneath them once a week and see what has come to shelter there or warm up. You could find anything from an ant nest to slow-worms or a family of voles or shrews. But slugs, earwigs and centipedes are more likely.

A log pile makes a perfect home for beetles and woodlice.

- Plant insect-friendly plants – these can be wildflowers, but older varieties of garden flowers are also good sources of nectar for butterflies and bees. Many insects will need different plants in their younger stages – especially nettles and other wild plants.

  - Leave a strip of lawn to grow taller and plant meadow plants in there. Leave them long enough to set their seeds, but mow it in July or August when the seeds have ripened and fallen off.

  - Don't be too tidy – seed heads and dead plants are often food for birds in their own right, but may also house insects, from earwigs to ladybirds.

  - Put up nestboxes for birds and bees and roosting boxes for bats and hedgehogs.

Let a bit of your lawn grow wild.

Widening your interest

Watching wildlife is a great activity because you can do it on your own, with one or two friends, or in much bigger groups. You can also combine it with other activities to increase your wildlife watching time. If you are waiting to bat at a school rounders game, can you count the swifts flying over, hear skylarks or count bumblebees on the clover?

Spread the word

If you do any of these things, then it's really good to tell people about them. Spotting and counting wildlife is really important in nature conservation. We have to know what's out there to decide if it needs any help – so wildlife watchers are always doing surveys. And it's people like you, enjoying wildlife for its own sake, who are the foundation of it all.

There is no end to the amount of wildlife that people would like you to look out for: birds, bats, basking sharks, butterflies and moths, dormice, jellyfish, glow worms and sulphur tuft, to name a few. In short, if you look for something, someone will want to know about it, whether you have found it or not.

Share what you have seen – it can help wildlife.

158

A group of friends who watch wildlife will never be bored!

Get involved

Some of the groups that regularly ask for volunteer surveyors include the RSPB, BTO, Plantlife, The Mammal Society, BugLife, Butterfly Conservation, Woodland Trust and local Wildlife Trusts. You often only need to identify one species to take part, and you would be told just what to do.

Buglife - www.buglife.org.uk

Ispot - www.ispot.org.uk

Natural History Museum - www.nhm.ac.uk

Plantlife - www.plantlife.org.uk

The RSPB - www.rspb.org.uk

The Wildlife Trusts - www.wildlifetrusts.org

Woodland Trust - www.woodlandtrust.org.uk

Habitats

The word 'habitat' means the type of place where an animal or plant normally lives. Woodlands, lakes and gardens are all habitats.

However, usually we will need to go into more detail than that. We may talk about oak woodland, which will have mainly oak trees, but will have plenty of other plants growing there as well. We may make sure we mention if it's a shallow or deep lake because they are likely to have different animals living in them – you won't find many diving ducks on a lake that would be shallow enough for a swan to reach the plants on the bottom. And gardens can be very different types of habitat depending on how they are looked after and where they are.

Remember though, animals and plants can view their own habitats very differently to us. A caterpillar munching away on an oak leaf in a garden may be just as happy as if it were in an ancient woodland. To that caterpillar, one oak tree is a habitat all of its own!

Specialist or generalist?

Some animals and plants are only found in one habitat. You won't find a limpet away from seashore rocks, for example. These animals and plants are called 'specialists'. You can find others in all sorts of places. Wrens or foxes will live on heathlands, upland moors, gardens, woodlands and even on the seashore. We call these 'generalists'. You, as a human being, are the ultimate generalist! People get everywhere.

A limpet is a specialist.

And something as big as an eagle may live in a huge area that covers bare mountain tops, heather moorland and even down into woodland. Even if the eagle doesn't need the woodland, some of its prey, such as red deer, may.

160

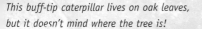

This buff-tip caterpillar lives on oak leaves,
but it doesn't mind where the tree is!

Scale

All this means that you have to think
about the scale when thinking about
habitats, and that will help you to see
more wildlife. If you are interested in
millipedes, for example, it's no use going
to a woodland and wandering around
hoping to spot one. You need to know
that they like to live under logs and
stones in damp places. That may be in
a woodland, but there are other places
where a suitable millipede habitat may
be found, such as in your own garden.

Some of the smallest habitats, such as
under a rock, are the least noticed and
are unspoiled, so be especially careful
when investigating that you don't upset
what lives there.

*What would you find
living in this habitat?*

161

Cliffs

Cliffs are fantastic but often dangerous places – for both people and wildlife. Many birds choose to nest on cliffs because they are so hard for predators to get to, and it is easy to take off from a cliff. This also makes them one of the country's most unspoilt habitats, but not always the oldest. The famous white chalk cliffs of Dover stay white because of frequent rock falls. Before plants have a chance to grow on the cliff face, it crumbles away, revealing more fresh clean chalk.

Sea cliffs are not only great places to spot the wildlife that lives on the cliffs, but also good places to watch for wildlife out at sea. Not only can you see farther out to sea from a high place, but you can also look into the dips and troughs of the waves that may hide passing ducks or dolphins from beach watchers. Some people spend hours watching the sea from cliff tops. It's not for everyone, but these seawatchers spot wildlife that no one else ever sees.

Don't forget that some rocks are also great for fossils, so beaches below the cliffs are good places to look for these, especially after fresh rock falls from the winter storms. Pay attention to any safety notices though.

On the cliff

Cliffs often have interesting plants and lichens growing on them, but you will need binoculars to get a good look at the best ones because they will be out of reach.

As well as the seabirds that nest on cliffs, this habitat is great for the world's fastest bird, the peregrine falcon. These fabulous birds swoop down over the rocks after an unsuspecting pigeon or jackdaw, and are so well-adapted to cliffs that they can be found in many man-made inland cliff sites. Man-made cliffs? You know them as skyscrapers or cathedrals in our towns and cities.

The white cliffs of Dover are made of crumbly chalk.

Rocky coasts, with their mix of sandy bays, rocky outcrops and rockpools, are fantastic places for wildlife. Even before you delve into the rockpools themselves, you will see how the wildlife positions itself in relation to the sea. At the very top of the beach, where there may be the occasional bit of salt spray from the waves, you may find sea-pink flowers and there will be different lichens on the rocks at the top of the beach than there are a bit lower down.

Farther down you will find the first of the shells, probably barnacles and a few periwinkles. Lower still there will be topshells and mussels, but all of these need to be covered by the tide occasionally because they only feed when they are covered with water. And at the bottom of the beach, only exposed at the lowest tides, you may see jelly-like blobs on the rocks. These are sea anemones.

Rockpools

This is the rockpool zone. There will be a mix of creatures that always live there and others that get trapped by each tide. Almost the whole community can change twice a day as the tide ebbs and flows.

When it comes to looking in the pools themselves, the same applies as for ponds – try to keep still and let the wildlife come out – and wear polarising sunglasses to cut out reflections. The rockpool residents, especially some of the shore crabs and larger shannies, will usually have a favourite ledge or stone to hide under. If you disturb them with your pond net, it is kindest to put them back where you found them.

When looking in rockpools, try to keep your shadow off the water.

163

Sandy beaches

Everyone loves a sandy beach, but they can often seem a bit lifeless for wildlife. Shingle beaches may look even worse. There are several reasons for this: sandy beaches are often crowded with people who accidentally frighten the wildlife away; much of it stays hidden under the sand until the tide comes in; and there really isn't as much to see on a sandy beach as on a rocky one.

The sand on our sandy beaches is made from rocks and pebbles, ground up by the tide. (In tropical countries, the white sand is made from ground-up coral and parrotfish poo!)

Sandy beach tips

A worm cast from a ragworm.

- Try to get there early, before other people have scared off the birds. You may see wading birds along the edge of the sea, and gulls bobbing about just off shore.

- Look along the tideline carefully. There will be interesting dead things washed up, but also living creatures, from sandhoppers and sea slaters to rock pipits and common shrews.

- If there is anyone digging for fishing bait down at the water's edge, ask if you can see what they have dug up – lugworms and ragworms are fascinating in their own right.

- Some beaches may have seals on – don't approach too close if you find one.

- Spend a bit of time looking at the shells that have washed up.

If you see seals, don't disturb them.

Sand dunes

In some places, the sea is washing more and more sand up on to the land. When this happens, sand dunes may form. In time, special plants start to grow on the dunes and this stops the sand from shifting. Marram grass is the most important of these grasses. It's really spiky!

Behind the dunes, wet marshy areas called dune 'slacks' may develop and these can hold amazing wildlife that is found nowhere else.

Sand dunes are great for seeing animal tracks, especially if the sand is wet. Look out for signs of foxes and rabbits and even toads in the slacks.

Sea buckthorn bushes, with their bright orange berries, may hold fieldfares, redwings and other migrant birds, and unusual plants such as sea spurge may live here.

The sandhill rustic moth lives in the dunes, along with wildflowers such as the early gentian. You might find red toadstools in the autumn.

Look for tracks and flowers in the dunes.

165

Mudflats and estuaries

You may be surprised at how fantastic these grey, muddy places are for wildlife. They are among our last truly wild big habitats. They are places of change – from river freshwater to sea saltwater. And wherever there is change there are opportunities for wildlife to get a foothold.

The biggest estuaries, such as Morecambe Bay in northwest England and The Wash in eastern England, hold thousands of birds all year around. But those birds change almost daily, making these tremendously exciting places for naturalists.

Huge numbers of waders pass through estuaries on their way to or from their breeding grounds. Many others spend the winter on the estuaries along with thousands of ducks and geese.

Estuary treasure

These birds come to feed on the invisible riches of estuaries, which are the millions of tiny worms and shellfish living in the mud and washed in by the tide. Along with heathlands, these are among our most underrated habitats, but not by naturalists.

Estuaries are famous for birds, but they may also hold otters, seals, flatfish, crabs and tonnes of shellfish – remember that bird food may be wildlife, too!

Don't forget to look in the mud for worms and shellfish!

A redshank on an estuary.

Machair

Shush! Don't tell too many people, but machair ('mak-kair') is one of Scotland's best-kept secrets. Machair is the low strip of fertile ground that forms between the sea and the peat bogs on some Scottish islands. The seashell soil balances the acid from the peat to make a fantastic growing medium for wildflowers. And where there are wildflowers there will also be wild animals.

Most of these Scottish islands don't have ground predators such as stoats, weasels and hedgehogs, so the machair is a safe place for nesting birds such as twites, corncrakes, dunlins and ringed plovers.

Machair is a great place to see wildflowers.

The plants are home to exciting insects, such as a bee called the northern colletes, the belted beauty moth and the great yellow bumblebee.

Lots of wildlife

The rare sand lizard lives in the machair on the island of Coll and otters pass through on their way to the coast. For a few short weeks of summer, the colourful strip of machair flowers is among the best in Europe. It is full of yellow rattle, wild thyme, birds-foot trefoil, harebells and even its own special marsh orchid that is found nowhere else.

Maintaining machair

Machair is so rare partly because it needs the right conditions to grow, but also because it needs people and our grazing animals to keep it in check. As with many other habitats that look completely natural, human influence is important and the small farming and crofting communities that live there can keep it just right.

Saltmarsh

Saltmarshes are flat areas mainly covered by the sea at high tide but revealing a network of muddy creeks and pools as the tide retreats. They can be vital for breeding and wintering wading birds and also have their own special plant life that has to cope with spending some of its time under seawater – being nibbled by fish and crabs – some in the open air and some under rain. Sea lavender and samphire are typical saltmarsh plants, with annual seablite on the slightly higher ground.

The most typical bird on the saltmarsh is the redshank, which loudly warns everything else that you are coming. Saltmarshes can have a surprising number of creatures living there, such as brown hares and lizards, and winter visiting birds such as snow buntings, shore and skylarks and linnets.

Bird life

Saltmarshes are great for wildfowl, including wigeons, teals and brent geese. They are also great places to see birds of prey such as marsh harriers, short-eared owls and even peregrines looking for a duck dinner.

They are not the easiest places to watch wildlife, but a walk along the edge of a saltmarsh as the tide is coming in and pushing wildlife out of the creeks can be very rewarding.

Look out for short-eared owls on a saltmarsh.

The creeks and pools of a saltmarsh attract a lot of wildlife.

The sea around us may look to be all the same – big, wet and cold, but it is really a whole range of habitats that run into one another. Different depths of water and whether the bottom is sandy or rocky, how rough it usually is, how warm it is and how far from land all make a difference to what lives there.

The warm currents called the Gulf Stream that flow up the west coast of Britain and Ireland, keep the water there warmer than in the east. But our strong westerly winds make western seas rougher.

From land, we can sometimes tell what the sea is like by watching the wildlife. If you see a flock of eider ducks, for example, you can be sure there are mussel beds underneath the water, and it is probably less than 10m deep.

There may well be a mussel bed under these eider ducks.

Lakes

Big lakes can often be a bit disappointing for the wildlife watcher. The wildlife is there, but most of it will be under water or staying out in the middle where it feels safe. You are often best looking around the edges, especially if there is any marshy land or reeds growing there.

However, some of our big lakes do have special fish, found nowhere else, and they can have lots of ducks and geese, especially in the winter.

Lake plants

Don't forget to look at the plants growing around and in a big lake. Some of these can be special. Those growing round the edge range from big willows and reeds down to little submerged plants, from flowering plants that keep their leaves submerged but stick their flowers up into the air to attract insects, to algae and mosses.

Many of these have to cope with drying out if the edge of the lake dries up in summer, or trying to get enough light as the water deepens around them. They also have to cope with being buffeted by waves, eaten and trampled by animals and changes in the water caused by pollution, especially farm chemicals washed into the water. It's not an easy life!

Grey herons stand at the edge of a lake.

Canals are usually sections of a river that people have straightened, deepened and slowed down to make them suitable for river traffic. Canals have tow paths that you can walk down, and often provide a bit of greenery in a city. The downside is that the bankside vegetation that would support all sorts of wildlife has usually been cut back, the water is likely to be murky and there may be a lot of other people around putting the wildlife off. It doesn't mean the wildlife isn't there – there will be fish, probably kingfishers and certainly moorhens and dragonflies around.

River life

Rivers are much more variable and much more exciting. Young rivers, high in the hills, will be small, fast-flowing and clear. As they work their way to the sea, they will go through rough and smooth patches, called pools and 'riffles', which hold different wildlife, before becoming wide, slow rivers, with reeds and other bankside vegetation.

The age and speed of the river makes a difference to what wildlife you will see. For example, dippers will be in the faster upper reaches, and kingfishers farther down where the water is clearer. You may find stonefly larvae in the oxygen-rich upper reaches, but more mayflies and damselflies farther down.

Some wildlife, such as salmon and eels, head right up from the sea to high pools. There is always something to see near a river.

Look for dippers in the upper reaches.

Reedbeds

Reedbeds are home to some great creatures. In the summer, you can see sedge warblers in any summer reedbed, and reed warblers in the southern ones, but you could be really lucky and see a bearded tit or even a bittern as well. Marsh harriers may be patrolling overhead, and water rails may be squealing from the reeds.

In early autumn, thousands of swallows and martins flock to reedbeds to spend the night. Even in winter, there will be starlings and reed buntings, and perhaps a barn owl hunting overhead.

But it's not just birds. Reedbeds are important places for water voles, otters, raft spiders, various rare moths, eels, frogs and even harvest mice with their tiny ball nests.

The reeds

Reedbeds are watery places, dominated by mainly one species of plant. You guessed it, the common reed. But drier parts of reedbeds contain more special wildflowers, from hemp agrimony to yellow iris.

The reeds grow to 3m tall and die back every year. The dead reeds don't rot away as quickly as the new ones grow, so they build up. This means that reedbeds are always slowly drying out, making it easier for trees to grow there. Eventually, they would become willow woodland if left on their own. Luckily, most big reedbeds are now looked after for wildlife – and for people to harvest the reeds to make thatched roofs – so as long as we keep supporting wildlife charities, reedbeds and their special wildlife should be safe.

Reeds grow to 3m tall.

Fen, marsh and wetland

Almost all these areas are now nature reserves, and with good reason. Wetlands have more wildlife of a greater range than any other habitat. That's because they have such variety, from willow trees, nettles and iris beds, to rough grassland and reedbed, muddy edges and open water of assorted depths. Just think of all the different animals and plants that can make a home in such places. Some birds will be found nowhere else, such as bitterns, marsh harriers and bearded tits, but others like barn owls or wrens will live here as well as many other places.

A few mammals, like water voles and otters, rely on watery places, but wetlands are also great places for seeing deer and even small mammals such as field voles.

Some insects live in wetlands and nowhere else, such as the Fenn's wainscot moth or the rare swallowtail butterfly. But they are good places to see much more common butterflies too, as well as dragonflies.

Places of change

One of the best things about wetlands is that they are always changing. They attract migrant birds, have a range of wildflowers and insects that are very seasonal and change with the weather, time of day and time of year. You never know exactly what to expect. But if you visit on a quiet day for your chosen type of wildlife, you can usually find something else to enjoy instead.

A swallowtail butterfly can only be seen in wetlands.

Ponds

Garden ponds, farm ponds, village duck ponds – all have wildlife worth looking at. Generally, the bigger, deeper and quieter the pond the more wildlife you will find. The fewer fish the better, too, unless you want to watch the fish themselves.

When you want to investigate a pond, it's really tempting to rush straight up to it with a pond net and see what you can catch. It's much better to sneak up carefully though and to try to have a look first, preferably without appearing on the pond creature's skyline. Then remain still and watch for a while.

You may see birds come to drink or bathe, or mammals coming to drink. You will probably start to see pond skaters on the surface, perhaps also water boatmen or three-tailed mayfly larvae walking along the bottom and even sticklebacks. As soon as you stick a net in, much of this will try to escape, but pond dipping is still one of the best ways to see what's in there.

Keep an eye out for frogs in your local ponds.

Pond dipping
Also works for rockpools, canals, slow rivers and lakes

The most important thing when dipping a pond is to stay safe. So cover up any cuts with a waterproof plaster, be careful not to poke anyone with your net, and, above all, don't fall in!

Before you dip your net in the water, collect a bit of the water in a tray or sandwich box. This is to keep the creatures in while you look at them. They won't want to be out of the water for long, so do this before you put your net in.

Next, sweep the net in long, smooth, slow movements under the water. Take your net out and immediately empty its contents into the tray – before you have tried to look in your dripping net.

Let the water in the tray settle and see what you can see swimming around. You can then catch the creatures in a plastic spoon in the tray.

Finally, empty the tray back into the pond by submerging it, not by pouring from waist height. Think of the headache that your poor creatures will get otherwise!

Try not to cast a shadow on the water.

Mountain and moorland

Big, windswept mountain landscapes are fantastic places, but not always easy for wildlife watchers. There are plenty of special creatures that live in the uplands, but the larger animals can be hard to creep up on because they can see you coming from a long way off.

Even though they can look bleak, mountain habitats include ponds, rivers, bogs, dry moorland, bare rocks and a lot of space. Look at it all in detail to get the best of it, rather than simply admiring the landscape.

Mountain wildlife

Most of the uplands have red deer, and there are mountain hares which turn white in winter on northern uplands. Breeding birds include the merlin, our smallest falcon, and the magnificent golden eagle, as well as nesting golden plovers, curlews, red grouse, hen harriers and ptarmigans, and there will be meadow pipits everywhere.

Red deer can be seen in most upland areas.

Mountain insects include the mountain ringlet butterfly, golden-ringed dragonfly and emperor moth, and don't forget to look at the plants.

Bilberries go by a variety of names that reflect their importance for people. You will also find heather and bracken, and cotton-grass and moor grass, and because the soils are usually rather poor, insectivorous plants that add to their diet by flycatching – look for sticky sundews and butterworts.

Be prepared

The effect of weather on mountain landscapes can be dramatic, and they can be remote places, so never explore these places on your own and without knowing what the weather has in store. It's not unknown for beautiful purple heathers on a clear morning to be covered in snow by the afternoon!

It's not surprising, then, then that much of the wildlife that can move will head downhill or move further south for the winter.

Lowland heath

Lowland heath is a special habitat that the UK has more of than anywhere else, but at first sight it can look rather boring. The main plants are gorse and various heathers, but if not managed it quickly fuzzes up with broom, Scots pine and silver birch trees. Much of the special wildlife of lowland heath needs wide open spaces without trees that predators will use as watch points. This means that heathland conservation often involves removing thousands of tree seedlings.

Heathlands are great places for dragonflies and butterflies. All our reptiles live on southern heaths. They are great places for birds such as Dartford warblers, woodlarks, nightjars and hobbies, and may have roe and the introduced sika deer.

Under threat

Lowland heathlands are semi-natural habitats. That means that they have developed over thousands of years of interaction between people, their animals and wildlife. People cleared trees from the areas and then grazed them with sheep or goats. This gradually made heathlands open up and created the right conditions for the special plants and the animals that like to eat them. Because people don't use heathlands for grazing so much these days, the trees are more likely to grow back, which would be bad news for the wildlife that lives there.

Nightjars are just one of the birds you might see here.

Forest

The New Forest in Hampshire in southern England is the biggest area of forest that we have, and it's a fantastic place for people and for wildlife. Forest isn't just another word for a woodland. There are trees, but there are also wide open places, areas of heathland and rivers. To be called a forest, the land area has to be large and have at least one-fifth covered with trees.

Forests can be great for wildlife that may otherwise struggle to fit onto our crowded islands, because this gives them a range of habitats. Birds, including honey buzzards, redstarts and wood warblers, depend on forested areas. Forests were originally places for hunting deer, and various species of deer still live here, including red and fallow.

Forests are great places for fungi, from the rare and much sought-after truffles to the fly agaric. And with this range of different habitats within a forest, there is no end to the number of insects you can find in the summer, day or night.

Forests cover large areas and have lots of trees.

A fallow deer.

178

Woodland edges give wildlife watchers the best of both worlds. The edges of habitats are often the best bits, and can be easier to watch than the middle of a thick woodland. Many creatures move between one habitat and another. For example, rabbits and buzzards may both feed in the open but retreat to woodland edges to sleep. Hedgehogs, badgers and foxes may also come out of the woodland to feed before heading back to the shelter of woodlands during the day.

Badgers usually come out of woodland at night.

A lighter place

The edges of woodlands can also be more interesting for plants and insects because they get more light than farther into the wood. You can often notice that woodland flowers are richer and flower earlier around the edges than in the middle. Plants such as red campion and cuckoo pint will often be nearer the edges.

The edges of older woodlands were often hedges planted to keep farm animals out of the wood (or sometimes in). This means you may find hedgerow trees such as hawthorn or spindle more at the edge of the woodland than inside. It also means the edges may be bushier, so you may be able to find garden warblers, blackcaps, and lesser whitethroats here more than in the middle.

Coniferous woodland

Most coniferous woodland is dense plantations for timber, often too closely packed for light to reach the ground. However, there are a few remnants of the original native pinewoods of Scotland. These have their own special wildlife, from twin-flowers to crested tits and red squirrels.

If the only conifer woods you find are densely planted, you can still find some wildlife. Look for the thinner areas, and look along paths and tracks. There are likely to be coal tits and goldcrests in the treetops and, if you are really lucky, crossbills.

On the ground, look for big living heaps of pine needles. These will be wood ant nests. You will see trails of ants going to and fro, possibly carrying caterpillars or other insect food.

The youngest areas of pines and the clearfell areas where the trees have been recently harvested can be some of the best places for wildlife – short-eared owls and roe deer in the clear fell and tree pipits, woodlarks and adders in the bare areas. On summer evenings, look for nightjars, woodcocks and glow-worms.

Look for red squirrels in the north.

Many pinewoods are too thick and dark to allow much wildlife to live there.

Thousands of years ago, most of the country was covered in woodland, especially oak and beech trees. Most of this was cleared away in the Bronze Age – can you imagine cutting down a huge tree with an axe you have made from stone with an antler handle? A few old pieces of woodland haven't been cut down for at least 400 years. We call these ancient woodlands and they are some of the best places in the UK for wildlife.

Woodland birds, such as woodpeckers, treecreepers and tawny owls live here, but so do dormice, roe deer, speckled wood butterflies, bluebells, primroses and King Alfred's cake fungi.

Newer woodland

Woodland that has been cut down at some point but then has been allowed to grow again can still be great for wildlife. You can often tell this sort of woodland because all the big trees may look to be about the same size and thickness. They may have been replanted 100 years ago after the old woodland had been removed to use as timber in World War 1.

Tawny owls and great spotted woodpeckers both live in woodland.

Meadow, pasture and downland

Don't be fooled into thinking that all open grass fields are the same. In general, the oldest ones that have had the least fertiliser put on them and have had just the right number of animals grazing them are the best. These are the downlands and wildflower meadows. In June they can be alive with butterflies, orchids and beetles.

Greener grassland that has had more grazing may still have wildlife, especially in neglected corners, but is likely to be poorer – the greener the grass, the fewer species it is likely to hold.

Grassland animals

The pyramidal orchid is a favourite with the day-flying burnet moth.

Cows and sheep graze on grasslands. They can attract their own wildlife. Look for magpies trying to steal wool from sheep's backs to line their nests. Or swallows flying around cows looking for flies. Watch for wagtails and starlings grabbing insects that have been disturbed as the cows walk about.

You may also see brown hares in the fields – the larger the field the better for them – but not for other wildlife.

Grazing cattle attract their own wildlife!

Arable farmland

This is land that is used for growing plant crops for people to eat or to feed to farm animals. Crops include wheat and barley, oil seed rape and field beans, sugar-beet, potatoes, carrots and plenty of others. These fields may be surrounded by hedges or fences and come in lots of different sizes.

In general, smaller fields are better for wildlife, especially if there are lots of different types of crop planted next to one another. Bigger fields also often contain only the crop, and no seed-filled weeds or insects for wildlife to eat.

Out in the open

Some species cling to the edges of fields, but others prefer the open spaces so that they can see predators coming. Skylarks, for example, like to nest in the middle of fields. When the crop has grown tall, it's often hard to spot much wildlife in it, but as the crop starts to grow or just after it has been harvested you may have more luck.

Look for partridges and pheasants in fields and kestrels hovering overhead. Rooks, jackdaws and gulls favour ploughed fields. Rabbits can be found around the edges, and brown hares in the middle of the field. Deer or foxes can also often be seen passing through.

On the edge

Sometimes you will find a wildlife-rich strip around the edge of the field. This may be a home for beetles, skipper butterflies and wildflowers.

Skylarks are among the few species that like big fields.

Hedgerows

In most cases, garden hedges are planted from just one type of bush. However, hedges in the countryside tend to be much more interesting. Some countryside hedges are among the oldest features in a landscape, especially if they form a boundary between two landowners. And the older, taller and thicker they are, the better they are for wildlife.

To work out roughly how old a countryside hedge is, count the number of tree species in about 30 big paces and multiply by 100. If the hedge contains mainly hawthorn, it was probably planted in the 18th or early 19th century.

Some hedges are so old that they are just thin strips of ancient woodland. These can have fascinating flowers, including bluebells and Solomon's seal, along with climbers such as honeysuckle and old-man's beard. Look out for fruit trees such as damsons and crab apples here too.

Wildlife-friendly

All these plants mean that hedges can be great for wildlife. Look for nesting yellowhammers and whitethroats in the summer, feeding redwings and fieldfares in the winter, and small mammals such as bank voles and shrews at any time of year.

Some insects are particularly associated with hedges, such as the very rare black hairstreak butterfly which lives on blackthorn.

As well as their resident and visiting wildlife, hedges provide safe corridors for wildlife to travel between otherwise separate pieces of woodland – think of them as nature's cycle paths. You can sometimes see wild animals crossing at gateways, going from one hedge to the next.

Old and thick hedges provide food and shelter for a lot of wildlife.

Parks and gardens

Just because somewhere looks nice and tidy for people doesn't mean it won't work for wildlife. It's true that many parks and gardens aren't brilliant for wildflowers because any that appear get pulled out as weeds. But there is usually a forgotten corner with a few weeds growing through, or that hasn't had too many garden chemicals thrown on it. These are the places to look first for interesting minibeasts, which, in turn, provide food for other garden wildlife such as hedgehogs and robins.

However, a lot of garden wildlife simply goes unnoticed. Over 100 different types of moths visit most gardens every year, and garden soil can contain all sorts of goodies.

Also garden flowers can be full of nectar. Simpler, older varieties of flowers are often better than some of the more modern ones, and these will attract butterflies.

Tidy places

Many town or city parks look too tidy for much wildlife. Some will have old trees that have their own wildlife. Others may have ponds and lakes. However, whatever is there, some form of wildlife will usually move into it.

Country parks are often more interesting for wildlife.

Remember though, make sure that you have permission to look in any gardens and don't go wandering in areas of parkland on your own.

Even in the tidiest park, you'll find some wildlife.

Bees visit nectar-rich garden flowers.

Urban environments

Towns and cities can be great places for watching wildlife. In some places they are even better than the surrounding countryside because parks, gardens and waste ground provide a range of habitats that may no longer exist elsewhere in the area.

In general, if you are looking for wildlife in towns and cities, try to find the oldest, most run-down and wettest parts of town. Tidy modern places have less wildlife.

Almost every town river and canal will have its fish and water life. Park lakes and streams and rivers running through towns are great for birds, and will have plants that you won't find anywhere else.

On buildings

Some urban wildlife depends on buildings, from nesting swifts and house sparrows to roosting bats and garden hedgehogs. Old-fashioned sewage works, usually on the edge of town, provide some of the best places inland to see wading birds and the first swallows migrating through. Pied wagtails and starlings may roost in towns in winter because they will be warmer than the countryside.

Tall city buildings can provide nesting sites for birds of prey, including kestrels and peregrines, and old churchyards, especially the neglected corners, can have all sorts of wildflowers and insects. Don't forget to look at the lichens on the gravestones themselves – the dates will tell you how old the lichens could be.

Any cracks in pavements or walls will soon be colonised by wildflowers. Don't just think of them as weeds – they may have been around since before the city was built.

Keep your eyes open

The key for the urban wildlife watcher is just to keep your eyes open. You may spot gulls flying overhead on their way to roost for the night, ladybirds and zebra spiders on the walls and windowsills – and even moths and other insects splattered on the front number plates of cars in the supermarket car park!

*House sparrows
depend on buildings.*

Most wildlife lives outdoors, but you will be able to find something alive in any home, however clean and tidy it is. There will be spiders, carpet mites and beetles, perhaps dog or cat fleas, the odd sleeping ladybird and lacewing, and maybe even mice. If your home isn't centrally heated, you may find silverfish, and perhaps even woodlice or slugs in damper patches. Occasionally a trail of ants may get in.

Your garage or shed is likely to have all these and more. If you leave windows open in the summer, all sorts of things may fly in!

Some wildlife, such as the daddy long-legs spider, is only ever found indoors in the UK! It usually lives in warmer climates farther south, but can survive here because we heat our homes to make them comfortable to live in.

If you get any new houseplants, you are likely to bring in more new animals. There may be tiny slugs that creep out of the soil. Very occasionally you may even find an exotic caterpillar in your shop-bought salad!

This daddy long-legs spider would not survive outside.

Wildlife everywhere

Wildlife really is everywhere. It's often a nuisance in the home – especially the beetle grubs or tiny moth caterpillars that eat natural fabrics or stored foods – but isn't it also amazing that such creatures choose to move in with us?

So before you decide to evict a newcomer from your home, take a good look at it, find out a bit more about it and enjoy it for its own sake. It's alive, it's here and it's fascinating!

Mammals

Did you know you're a mammal? Humans are mammals. We have things in common with all other mammals that help tell us apart from other creatures.

About mammals

- Mammals have hair. Fur is just a special sort of hair that traps more heat by having a thick under layer and then 'guard' hairs over it to keep warm air in.

- Mammals have moveable lips – this helps us to eat and talk, and sometimes, for other mammals, to investigate their world. Watch how a rabbit uses its lips to hold grass while it is chewing it.

- Mammals have live, wriggling babies. We don't lay eggs.

- Mammals feed their young milk that their mothers make. You very rarely see this in the wild because mothers like to keep their babies away from prying eyes and teeth.

- Mammals, like birds, regulate their body temperature. This means that most of us keep going, whatever the weather! The only mammals in the UK that hibernate are bats, hedgehogs and dormice.

The UK has about 46 species of land mammals, ranging from pygmy shrews that are about 8cm long to red deer that may be over 200cm long. We also have 18 species of bats, breeding Atlantic grey and common seals, and over 20 different whales and dolphins that visit our seas. If you see more than five species of mammals in a day you are doing well.

Hedgehogs are one of the UK's only hibernating mammals.

If you want to get a decent view of bigger mammals, such as otters, deer and foxes, you will need to creep up on them very slowly and carefully. Mostly, you will catch a glimpse through binoculars if you are lucky, or will be able to spot them from a hide.

Top tips for mammal watching

- Dawn and dusk are the best times to see most mammals.

- Wear dull, non-rustly clothes and a hat with a brim so that you break up your outline and don't scare the creatures.

- Stay downwind of mammals when you can. They have a much better sense of smell than we do. To most mammals, you are still smelly even when you're clean!

- If you see a mammal, stop still, don't stare straight at it and don't point at it or it will run away.

- Keep low and off the skyline, don't approach in a straight line and move slowly and quietly.

- Small mammals can be easier to see because they don't recognise people. Again, keep still and look through binoculars.

- If you see a mink, stoat or weasel, try making squeaking noises to attract it. They will often come quite close. Do the same to a rabbit and it will run away!

Squeaking noises encourage weasels to come closer.

Going batty!

Most of the sounds that bats make are too high for people to hear. This sound is called ultrasound. You may hear the odd high-pitched squeak, but even then you will be missing most of it. This is where bat detectors come in.

Sound is really important for bats. They find their way around and hunt flying insects, mainly moths, by shouting at them and listening for the echo that bounces back. Bats can tell whether there is a tree in front or a juicy moth – handy! Each different type of bat calls at a different pitch and in a different way.

Bat detectors

Bat detectors pick up this high-pitched sound and translate it into lower noises that we can hear and use to identify the bats. The cheapest bat detectors cost £30-40, but are well worth putting on your Christmas list. As well as bats, they are great for listening to crickets and grasshoppers. Jangle a bunch of keys in front of a bat detector and be amazed at how much ultrasound they pick up.

A brown long-eared bat has big ears to catch sounds.

Bats

Our 18 bat species are our only flying mammals. They all hibernate in the winter when there are no flying insects for them to eat.

Brown long-eared bat (25cm wingspan)

Identification: Looks about the size of a starling in flight. Huge ears, nearly as long as its body, and big eyes (for a bat).

Behaviour: Flies quite slowly about 6m above the ground. Picks insects from tree leaves as well as catching them in flight.

Fact: Long-eared are much quieter than other bats so are hard to find with a bat detector.

Where to see it: Parks, gardens and woodland edges. Roosts in groups of up to 30 in trees or older buildings.

Don't confuse with: Other bats. But if you can see the ears, this bat is obvious.

Daubenton's bat (25cm wingspan)

Identification: Often called the water bat because it is usually seen low over calm, clear water – the smoother the better.

Behaviour: Catches insects hatching from still water – ponds, canals, and slow-moving rivers.

Fact: This bat was named in honour of an 18th Century French naturalist.

Where to see it: Look for open water near trees. They come out around an hour after sunset on summer nights.

Don't confuse with: Other bats, which look similar in flight. This is the main one that patrols over water.

Insect eaters

Worms and insects can feed much bigger animals, such as these.

Pygmy shrew (8.5mm, including tail)

Identification: A tiny, hyperactive grey-brown mammal with a long, flexible snout and short thick tail.

Behaviour: Munches its way through more than its own body weight of insects, spiders and woodlice every day.

Fact: This is our smallest mammal, but has one of our largest fleas living on it – it's bigger than the shrew's eye!

Where to see it: Pygmy shrews live all over the UK in long grass and wooded areas.

Don't confuse with: Common and water shrews, which are both larger. No other small mammals have such snuffly looking noses.

Hedgehog (Up to 30cm long)

Identification: Our only spiky mammal. Brown and round, but with surprisingly long legs when running.

Behaviour: Usually on short grass, in woodlands or on lawns, where it hunts for slugs, snails and earthworms to eat. Makes loud grunts and squeals in early summer.

Fact: Although hedgehogs famously hibernate, they may wake up several times in a winter and move house.

Where to see it: Suburban gardens, and woodland edges throughout the UK, except on a few remote islands.

Don't confuse with: Hedgehogs are unmistakable!

Rabbit and hares

Together, these long-legged jumpers are called lagomorphs. We have three species in the UK.

Rabbit (40cm)

Identification: Grey-brown and very rounded, with long back legs, long ears and big, alert eyes on the side of their head. A short white tail sticks up as they bound away.

Behaviour: Usually keeps within a few hundred metres of its burrow. Eats grass and crops. Left undisturbed, can sometimes be seen sunbathing, but usually comes out at dusk. Live in communities called warrens.

Fact: Generally silent, but squeals in distress. Males may thump the ground with their back legs to warn of approaching danger.

Where to see it: Almost anywhere that they can dig and find food, including sand dunes, woodland edges, hedgerows, large gardens and roadsides.

Don't confuse with: Hares, which are larger, have even longer back legs and black-tipped ears and black on the tail.

Brown hare (50-60cm)

Identification: More red brown than mountain hare (which turns white in winter), and much bigger and more angular than rabbits. Staring yellow eyes if you can get close enough to see.

Behaviour: Females can be seen fighting males off in the spring mating season, but often you will just see them sitting in fields. They are most active at night and are usually alone.

Fact: Brown hares can run at speeds of up to 45 mph. Brown hares spend the day in a slight dip in the ground called a form.

Where to see it: Wide open country, especially farmland.

Don't confuse with: Mountain hare, which is more rabbit-like and turns white in winter. It is also blue-grey in summer, except in Ireland, where it is brown!

193

Small rodents

Scurrying little vegetarians. Most don't live longer than a year.

Field vole (110mm long)

Identification: Small grey-brown and short tailed and round. Smaller eyes and shorter, blunter face than rats, mice or shrews.

Behaviour: Forms little tracks and runs in old damp grassland, where it spends most of its time eating grass.

Fact: There are more field voles in the UK than there are people.

Where to see it: Even though they are so common, your best chance of seeing a vole is either its remains in an owl pellet or by trapping, perhaps at a river bank.

Don't confuse with: Bank vole, which is redder and has a longer tail. Water vole is much larger and is usually seen swimming away.

Harvest mouse (50-70mm long)

Identification: Our smallest mouse has a tail that it can use as a gripping and climbing tool. It has hairy ears and a gingery colour.

Behaviour: Clambers through reeds and corn using its tail as an extra limb. Weaves a tennis-ball sized nest close to ground level.

Fact: Declined massively with changes in farming, so is now more common in reedbeds than in corn fields.

Where to see it: Mainly in England, from Yorkshire southwards. Look around the edges of cornfields and reedbeds for nests. The animals themselves stay well hidden.

Don't confuse with: Wood mouse. Its hairy ears and useful tail tell this apart.

Red squirrel and mole

Up in the trees or burrowing underground – these are perfectly adapted to their homes.

Red squirrel (35cm long including tail)

Identification: Red to grey brown on top and pale underneath with tufted ears (especially in winter) and a bushy red tail.

Behaviour: Mainly scampering around in pinewoods, but will also come to the ground and feed on peanuts in bird feeders. Active for most of the year.

Fact: Red squirrels are much rarer in Britain than they used to be, but are still the main squirrel in Ireland and most of mainland Europe.

Where to see it: Now mainly in Scotland and Ireland, but also in a few places in northern England and Wales, plus outposts on the Isle of Wight, and Brownsea Island in Dorset.

Don't confuse with: The much larger grey squirrel, which can look a bit brownish, but never so red as these.

Mole (12cm long)

Identification: Very short, black or grey fur, paddle-like feet, small eyes and a long snout. Surprisingly quick movements above ground.

Behaviour: Spends almost its whole life underground in tunnels, coming up only to avoid flooding or for young ones to find a new place to live.

Fact: Super-sized mole hills, called fortresses, may contain several nests and are often built on slightly higher ground to avoid flooding.

Where to see it: You can see evidence of moles in most habitats – mole hills and tunnels just breaking the surface sometimes, but not in Ireland. Seeing a live mole is quite rare.

Don't confuse with: Unmistakeable!

Carnivores

Fish and meat eaters have forward-facing eyes and sharp teeth for hunting.

Otter (up to 130cm long)

Identification: Bigger than many people think. Dark brown, sleek and streamlined. Short legs and a strong-looking tail. Noticeable hump at the hip.

Behaviour: Classic fish-eater, always in or near water. Often nocturnal on English rivers, but sometimes comes out during the day, especially on Scottish islands.

Voice: High-pitched squeaking sounds keep the family in contact, but often completely silent.

Where to see it: Now recorded in every county, but elusive.

Don't confuse with: The much bolder mink, which is much smaller, and has longer darker fur.

Fox (105cm long including 40cm tail)

Identification: Dog-like but with a lighter build and bushier tail. Orange-red fur above and white below. Tail has a white tip.

Behaviour: Hunters and scavengers, foxes will eat anything and live anywhere. They raise their cubs in a simple dug-out den, called an earth.

Voice: A barking yelp and various shrieks tell you that foxes are around.

Where to see it: Although there are far more foxes in the countryside than in towns and cities, the urban ones are often easier to see because they are less scared of people.

Don't confuse with: Medium-sized dogs, which can look similar, but are rarely as slender.

Badger (90cm long)

Identification: Stocky, short-legged. Grey above and black below with distinctive black-and-white head stripes.

Behaviour: Families live together and come out from their burrows, called a sett, at night to hunt worms and fruits.

Fact: There are about 200,000 badgers in the UK, but most people have never seen a live one.

Where to see it: Best seen by waiting quietly downwind of an active sett at dusk. Badgers live throughout the UK, especially where the ground is dry enough to dig burrows without their flooding.

Don't confuse with: Unmistakeable!

Polecat (50cm long including tail)

Identification: Short-legged and long tailed. These agile creatures have black-and tan fur and a dark bandit mask over a pale face.

Behaviour: Polecats are slim enough to hunt rabbits in their burrows, but they tend to hunt rats in the winter.

Fact: The polecat is the ancestor of the domestic ferret.

Where to see it: Polecats are spreading back through Britain (but they never lived in Ireland) and are usually shy. One or two people have set up watching schemes, but otherwise you will just have to be really lucky.

Don't confuse with: Domestic ferrets, which are the same species and may even be the same colour.

Wildcat (about 80cm including tail)

Identification: Like a large, stripy tabby cat, with a thick, blunt-tipped tail. Never tame enough to come for a stroke!

Behaviour: Very shy and generally nocturnal. These hunters rely on catching small mammals.

Fact: Wildcats used to live throughout Britain and Ireland but people either hunted them or removed their habitat.

Where to see it: These are really hard to spot, even in the Scottish Highlands where they live. You may see one in a zoo, but to find one in the wild is a once-in-a-lifetime treat.

Don't confuse with: Big domestic cats, which can look similar, but rarely so fierce.

For such fierce hunters, wildcats are very shy of people.

Seals

Sleek and streamlined for swimming and hunting fish – but faster on land than you might think.

Grey seal (up to 200cm long)

Identification: The larger of our two seals. Usually grey or brown and often spotty, but darker when wet. Looks down its arched Roman nose and opens and shuts its vertical nostrils.

Behaviour: Grey seals come ashore to breed in the autumn but spend most of their time at sea hunting fish.

Voice: Various snorts, grunts and long strained whistling calls can sound quite human from a distance.

Where to see it: Over half the world's grey seals live around our coasts, so they can pop up anywhere, but they have traditional pupping grounds, such as the Farne Islands and Blakeney Point that can best be visited on boat trips.

Don't confuse with: Common seal, which is smaller with a more dog-like face. If you see something at sea with a fin on its back, it's a fish, whale or dolphin.

Common seal (up to 150cm long)

Identification: The smaller of our two seals, with a dog-like face, long whiskers and finer spots. Its nostrils line up like the letter V.

Behaviour: Spends most of its time at sea, but comes ashore to have its pup and to moult its fur in the summer.

Voice: Sad singing that used to be thought of as mermaids.

Where to see it: Common seal is rarer in Britain than grey seal, but more common in Ireland. They visit traditional sites each year, sometimes with greys. Often seen off the coast, especially in Scotland.

Don't confuse with: Grey seals, which are bigger, blotchier and have vertical nostrils.

Whales and dolphins

Despite living at sea, these all have to come to the surface to breathe air – and sometimes we can see them.

Bottle-nosed dolphin (up to 4m long)

Identification: Dark grey, with a clear, but short 'beak' (really its mouth) and a tall fin on the centre of its back.

Behaviour: Usually in groups and generally seen jumping clear from the water. Dolphins spend their time hunting fish in groups.

Voice: Various high-pitched squeaks and whistles that we don't understand.

Where to see it: Your best bet is to either look from a high headland on a calm day or from a ferry. In a few places, such as the Moray Firth, groups of dolphins regularly come close to land.

Don't confuse with: Other dolphins. But this is the commonest of five species of dolphin that occur in UK waters.

Harbour porpoise (up to 1.8m long)

Identification: Dark with a short, blunt head. The fin on its back is quite short.

Behaviour: Usually breaks the water surface only to breathe, so rarely breaches. Hunts alone or in groups of up to five individuals, often near the shore.

Voice: As the name suggests, porpoises sometimes come into harbours or even up rivers.

Where to see it: You could be lucky from any of our coasts, but they are rarest in the Channel. They are most commonly seen in spring and summer.

Don't confuse with: Other dolphins and pilot whales. Look for the rounded head and small size.

Killer whale or Orca (around 7m long)

Identification: Black above and white below with a tall triangular dorsal fin and white patch above and behind the eye.

Behaviour: Social and intelligent killer of fish, birds and other sea mammals – but not humans so it is still safe to go into the water!

Voice: Very complex range of squeaks, clicks and whistles used to keep in touch with the rest of the family and to coordinate hunting.

Where to see it: Killer whales come to the waters of north and east Scotland regularly, but not predictably enough to plan a holiday around.

Don't confuse with: Unmistakeable if seen clearly, but pilot whale is a similar shape.

Minke whale (up to 9m long)

Identification: Quite small (for a whale!) and with a pointed snout. Dark back and pale belly, always with a white mark on its flippers.

Behaviour: Usually on its own, this whale visits our seas in search of a wide range of fish and crustaceans.

Voice: As loud as a jet aeroplane taking off, and similarly mechanical.

Where to see it: Whale watching trips from the Isle of Man and west Scotland are your best bet, along with longer ferry journeys. They rarely visit southern or eastern coasts.

Don't confuse with: Other similar whales, which are much larger. Pilot whales have a much more rounded head.

Deer

Nimble and built for running and jumping – to escape the wolves we no longer have.

Muntjac (1m long)

Identification: Our smallest deer. About the size of a Labrador dog, but darker, rounder, with spindly legs and very short tails. Short antlers and black stripes on the face.

Behaviour: Visits woodland and gardens where it can be quite bold and can wreak havoc with wildflowers.

Voice: A harsh, repeated bark, rather like a dog's, usually given at dusk or at night.

Where to see it: Along the edges of woodlands (and sometimes major roads) and in larger parks, gardens and churchyards.

Don't confuse with: A running dog or Chinese water deer, which are rarer and more ginger in colour than dark brown.

Red deer (up to 2.3m long)

Identification: Our biggest deer. Males, called stags, have huge spiky antlers. The females, called hinds, don't. Both are mainly a rich red-brown colour.

Behaviour: Usually in single-sex herds for most of the year, but males come together to fight for females in the autumn mating season, called the rut.

Voice: Rutting stags make loud bellowing calls.

Where to see it: Across moors and hills, especially across Scotland and south-west England, but also in deer parks in other places.

Don't confuse with: Sika deer, which look very similar and may interbreed with red deer. Fallow deer usually look spotty and have flatter antlers.

Look out for red deer in the Scottish Highlands

Reptiles and amphibians

These two groups are often talked about together, even though they are quite different. Our land reptiles are either snakes or lizards. There are also half a dozen sea turtles that visit occasionally, with leatherback being the most common. Our amphibians are frogs, toads or newts.

Snakes

We have only three native species of snake, the grass snake, the very rare smooth snake and the adder (or viper). The adder is our only venomous snake, but it very rarely bites people. It is much more likely to slither away or to hiss a warning if it is cornered.

Lizards

We have two native legged lizards, the common and sand lizards, plus the slow-worm. Slow-worms aren't worms and they aren't slow! They are legless lizards, which makes them look rather like snakes. They do, however have eyelids (snakes don't), and can drop their tail if they need to escape, just like their leggy relatives.

Amphibians

Reptiles have dry, scaly skin, but amphibians keep their skin damp and have to return to water to breed, even if they spend much of their time on land. Our amphibians with tails are the three newts, smooth or common newt, palmate newt, and great crested newt. They look like damp, slow-moving lizards. They are usually seen in ponds, but may spend the winter tucked under bark or in a wood pile.

Common frog and common toad are our most common tailless amphibians – but even they have tails as tadpoles. There is also the very rare natterjack toad that lives on coastal sand dune ponds.

Common lizards can sometimes be found warming up at the start of the day.

Look for newts in ponds in summer.

Cold-blooded creatures

If you were to take a frog's temperature on a cold day, it would be lower than on a hot day. However, yours wouldn't be, unless you were ill. This is why we call reptiles and amphibians cold-blooded. It just means they use the Sun's warmth to get them up to operating temperatures.

Morning watch

This is useful for us warm-blooded nature watchers because we can be up and active and looking for snakes before they have warmed up enough to slide away. Find a large, open, sheltered south-facing surface, such as a big stone or a log. Watch it carefully early on spring and summer mornings and you may be lucky enough to spot a reptile. Later in the day, it would hear you coming and have the energy to run away.

First thing in the morning, you may find a slow-worm or lizard warming up under a sheet of corrugated iron in long grass. If you can get hold of some black roofing felt, why not put some of that down in a hot spot in your garden and look under it in the morning?

A common toad uses the Sun's warmth to keep moving.

Water watching

Amphibians are also cold-blooded, so look for them in the warm shallows of lakes and ponds. Raising tadpoles from frogspawn is easy and fun and you should be able to get many through to tiny frog stage. Remember to release them back into the pond you caught them in to avoid spreading disease between ponds.

Newts are easily caught in pond nets and can be given a thorough examination in a dipping tray. Then let them go again unharmed.

205

Snakes and lizards

Smooth skinned and fast, these predators only come out in the summer.

Adder (up to 90cm long)

Identification: Quite a fat snake with bold zigzag marking all down the back. Can vary from almost black to very pale brown. No bright yellow collar.

Behaviour: Usually seen warming itself up in the mornings in a favoured sunny spot. Hunts small mammals and lizards.

Fact: This is our only venomous snake but it very rarely bites people. It prefers to escape. The bite is painful and serious but hardly ever kills people.

Where to see it: On heathland and grasslands throughout Britain, but sadly not in Ireland.

Don't confuse with: Grass snake, which is green with a yellow neck collar and usually seen in water. Smooth snake is very rare, is slimmer and usually has a line of spots down its back.

Common lizard (up to 15cm long)

Identification: Quite plain looking, usually brown, but sometimes grey or pale green. Thin stripes run down the sides of its body.

Behaviour: Runs very fast to catch insects to eat, but spends a lot of time watching and waiting, especially on old wood.

Fact: The lizard lives all the way north into the Arctic Circle.

Where to see it: Heathlands and old grasslands throughout the UK.

Don't confuse with: Sand lizard, which is much bigger and more colourful. Newts look damp and are very slow on land.

Amphibians

These creatures like to stay damp. They breathe through their skin as well as with their lungs.

Common frog (up to 9cm body length)

Identification: Mostly green or brown, with blotching, including a dark patch behind the eye. The back has a definite hump.

Behaviour: Frogs spend more time in wet grass than in ponds, but are expert swimmers, jumpers and fly catchers.

Fact: Mostly silent, but spring evening churring calls suggest that males are looking to mate. Only American frogs go 'ribbit'!

Where to see it: Garden ponds, lakes and wet moorlands throughout the UK. Frogs will lay their eggs, called spawn, in almost any puddle.

Don't confuse with: Toads, which have drier, lumpier skin, are generally plainer brown and lack the eye patch.

Great crested newt (up to 16cm long)

Identification: A big warty newt. Black or nearly so above and with orange spots underneath. Males are bigger and darker than females and have a spiky crest in the summer.

Behaviour: Outside the summer breeding season, newts are found under logs or in other damp places, but up to a mile from their ponds.

Fact: Each male crested newt has a unique pattern of spots on its tummy.

Where to see it: This is rare but found in some ponds almost all over England. It is rarer in Scotland and Wales and absent from Ireland.

Don't confuse with: Other newts, which are paler and smaller. Lizards are scaly and fast-moving.

Fish

All fish spend their entire lives in water, except for the odd leap here and there. They lay eggs and breathe through gills, and generally have streamlined bodies so that they can swim easily. Beyond that, there is huge variation. Fish are every bit as interesting as many other groups.

About fish

The most primitive fish are the sharks, skates and rays that live in the sea. Dogfish and porbeagle are our most common sharks, but they are tiny. We also have basking sharks up the west coast of Britain every summer. These are huge and harmless. Isn't it brilliant that the second biggest fish in the whole of the sea can be seen from our western cliff tops?

Flatfish are important for food for people, and our estuaries are flatfish breeding grounds. They are brilliant creatures. Many people will be familiar with them from big aquariums, but you can sometimes find baby flatfish in rockpools, or see them skitter away as you paddle slowly through the shallow water on a sandy beach.

Eels and salmon are two species that spend some of their time at sea and the rest – during their breeding season – in rivers. We also have many much smaller fish in our lakes, rivers and canals. However, a lot of anglers have released fish in these places for sport so their distribution is often not natural.

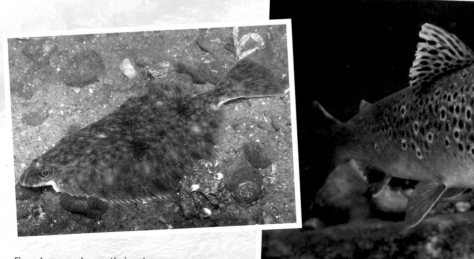

Flounders can change their colour to match their background.

Catching fish is more popular than watching them, but fish are fine creatures in their own right, if difficult to observe in the wild.

The easiest fish to spot while staying dry will usually be in clear shallow rivers or canals. You can sometimes see trout, pike, perch or even bream from a bridge.

Fish spotting tips

- Choose a bright day so that light penetrates the water.

- You may need to keep low down so that the fish doesn't spot you against the sky.

- Wear sunglasses with polarising lenses to cut through reflections on the water.

- Look for the smoothest water you can and a pale riverbed.

- If you catch minnows or sticklebacks – tiddlers – make sure to let them go where you found them when you have had a good look.

- Explore fish in seaside rockpools – you may find gobies, blennies and butterfish, baby flatfish and others trapped by the rising tide.

- In the sea, swim with a snorkel and mask over seaweed on an incoming tide and you may see wrasse, sea-pout and sand-eels. Don't do this alone, though. Also, remember only to do this on beaches where you know it is safe to swim.

Use a snorkel and mask to get a closer look at sea wildlife.

Some brown trouts spend time at sea, but they all breed in fresh water.

Freshwater fish

Always expect river fish to be facing upstream – they are streamlined to point into the current.

Pike (up to 1.5m long)

Identification: The streamlined shape, with a dorsal fin near to the tail and a huge toothy alligator grin, is distinctive, but expect the colours and patterns to vary.

Behaviour: Pike are fierce predators that spend a lot of time in the shallows of lakes and rivers, gradually creeping up on other fish before darting after them with lightning speed – exciting fish!

Fact: Pike can live for up to 30 years.

Where to see it: Lakes, reservoirs and slow-moving streams all over the UK. Look from bridges for the spear shape hanging still in the water.

Don't confuse with: The pike's body shape and patient watching are distinctive. Trout may look similar from above, but they are always moving.

Three-spined stickleback (8cm long)

Identification: These small fish have three spines sticking out of their back. Breeding males have red tummies and blue eyes.

Behaviour: Male sticklebacks defend a breeding territory, and invite females in to lay their eggs. It is the male who looks after the eggs.

Fact: The redder the male, the more successful he is likely to be.

Where to see it: Slow-moving streams and larger ponds, but also found in the sea.

Don't confuse with: 10-spined stickleback, which looks longer. Minnows lack the spines.

Seafish

Wildlife exists everywhere – even in your local chip shop!

Atlantic mackerel (20-50cm)

Identification: Silver-white below with blue-green stripes above. This animal is built for speed. Its fins even fold into streamlined slots when it wants to escape quickly.

Behaviour: Mackerel hunt together in huge schools that come close to land every summer to catch smaller fish and prawns.

Fact: Each female mackerel can lay over half a million eggs in a year.

Where to see it: These beautiful fish live all around our shores, which is why mackerel fishing trips are so common. You can often see dead ones in a fishmonger's display.

Don't confuse with: This is one of 10 species in the family that have been caught in British waters. Others include the famous blue-fin and skipjack tunas.

Basking shark (up to about 12m long)

Identification: A huge, harmless, dark grey shark, with a massive mouth that it holds open almost all the time. From land, you need to be sure that you can see both a dorsal fin (on its back) and the tail fin poking out of the water as the shark feeds on tiny creatures near the surface.

Behaviour: Basking sharks follow their food by migrating up the south and west coasts of Britain and Ireland in the summer before heading back out into the Atlantic for the rest of the year.

Fact: This is the second biggest fish in the sea (only the whale shark is bigger), but it eats some of the smallest creatures – just lots of them!

Where to see it: Cornish, Irish and Scottish headland. A few tourist boats search for them, but even they don't always find them.

Don't confuse with: Whales and dolphins, which only have one fin breaking the water surface.

Insects

Insects are all around us all the time, from the fleas on your dog to the moths at your windows on a summer evening. Insects are the most diverse group of creatures on the planet, but they all have a few things in common.

About insects

Insects have a clear three-part body plan: head, thorax and abdomen. The head is the sensory hub, where the eyes and the mouth are, the thorax is the segment where an insect's six legs, and also the wings that most of them have, grow from, and the abdomen is where digestion and reproduction occur. This body plan is probably easiest to see in ants, wasps and bees, but it is the same in other insects.

The study of insects is called entomology. There are still things about insects that are unknown to science that you can help discover. For example, we don't know what every UK caterpillar eats in the wild.

Insects have some of the most amazing lifestyles. There is the change from egg to caterpillar to chrysalis and flying adult that all our butterflies and moths go through. And what about the mayflies that live underwater as larvae for a year and then hatch, fly and mate in just a few hours before dying?

All insects have six legs and a head-thorax-abdomen body plan.

Insects take some outwitting! Three ways that insect watchers often use to find out which insects live in a place are with pooters, pitfall traps and tree-beating.

Pooter

A pooter is a handy device for capturing small insects unharmed and containing them while you have a good look. You can make one yourself easily, following this diagram:

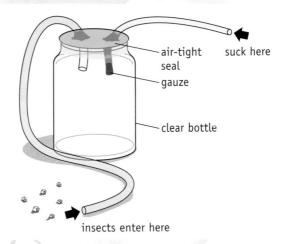

air-tight seal

suck here

gauze

clear bottle

insects enter here

Use it to suck up insects and spiders that are smaller than the entrance to the tube. Place your tube near the insect and take a sharp breath on the other tube. Don't blow – you will steam up the pot! Try to collect several similar insects together unless you want your pooter to become a battlefield of predator and prey.

Pitfall traps

Sink empty yoghurt pots into soil or a lawn right up to the brim. Leave them overnight and check in the morning to see what has fallen in. It's best to do this when you know there won't be any rain overnight. You can't be sure of catching swimmers!

Tree-beating

Lay an old sheet or open a large umbrella under a low branch and then knock the branch sharply. You'll take various minibeasts by surprise and they will drop off on to your sheet, where you can inspect them. Catch them with your pooter if you like.

Containers

You can buy tubes for holding insects, but the best thing is a bug-box. This has a magnifying glass built into the lid so that you can get a good look at your critter before letting it go. Getting an insect into a bug box isn't always easy. Try steering it in with a soft paintbrush.

Dragonflies

Fast-flying hunting insects with long bodies and clear wings that stick out sideways when they land.

Golden-ringed dragonfly (80mm long)

Identification: Our biggest dragonfly. Bright green eyes and black-and-yellow bands right up its body.

Behaviour: Often flying lazily over the streams where it lays its eggs, but also seen over heathlands. Sometimes it flies quite high, but its distinctive colours make it easy to spot.

Fact: The larva can live in a stream, mainly buried with only its head sticking out waiting for food to wander past, for up to five years before hatching as an adult dragonfly.

Where to see it: Anywhere in north, west or south Britain with acid soils. Heathlands and moorlands with shallow streams are favoured. Look for adults in your summer holidays.

Don't confuse with: This is the only dragonfly with this pattern, but there are other big blue or green ones.

Emperor dragonfly (78mm long)

Identification: A big and bulky-looking dragonfly, often looking a little droopy in flight. Both sexes have green bodies, but males have blue tails and females have green. Both have a black stripe down the tail.

Behaviour: Very powerful and always active. You won't see them perched often because they even eat in mid-air. Expect to see them zooming around over larger ponds, lakes and canals all summer.

Fact: This dragonfly defends a feeding territory against others of the same species, so you often see fights between rival males.

Where to see it: Over any large freshwater body in England, Wales and southern Scotland.

Don't confuse with: Similar hawker dragonflies. None of these have the black stripe running down their tail section.

Damselflies

Smaller, slow-motion dragonflies, with wings that lie along their body when they rest.

Common blue damselfly (33mm long)

Identification: Males are bright blue with less black than other similar species. Females may be either bright blue or dull green.

Behaviour: Flies over any lake, reservoir or pond in search of smaller insects to eat and other common blues to mate with.

Fact: This is the most common damselfly. Sometimes you can see hundreds of them together, but don't worry. They are completely harmless to people.

Where to see it: Over still water of almost any size through the UK, from May to October.

Don't confuse with: Other very similar damselflies, including azure damselfly, but this is the bluest of them all.

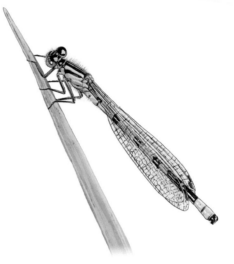

Banded agrion (48mm long)

Identification: The males of this large damselfly have a dark band through their wings that makes them flicker in flight. Females are metallic green and have dusky wings.

Behaviour: The males defend territories along slow-moving streams and canals, but sometimes group together and dance to impress females.

Fact: This damselfly can be found in suitable habitats right across the world to China.

Where to see it: Mainly slow rivers and canals with muddy bottoms throughout the UK. You rarely see it far from water.

Don't confuse with: Other green female damsels, which all have clear wings. The males' wing bars are unique.

Butterflies and moths

Butterflies and moths are all part of the group called Lepidoptera, which just means 'scaled wings'. Their wings are covered with tiny, powdery scales that give them colour. In time some of these wear off, giving older ones a tatty appearance.

About butterflies and moths

All butterflies and moths go through the same life cycle: they start as an egg, from which a caterpillar hatches out. This grows until it turns into a pupa, often called a chrysalis, which finally hatches as a flying adult which mates and lays more eggs. How long all this takes and what each creature does at these different stages of its life cycle is what makes the group interesting. Some butterflies and moths spend the winter as adults, for example, but others do so as eggs. Some moth caterpillars eat so much that they don't need to feed at all as adults, and some adult moths don't even have mouth parts at all!

All our butterflies are active during the daytime in spring or summer. Most moths come out on summer nights. However, there are more day-flying moths than there are butterflies in the UK, and you can see moths in every month of the year.

About 95% of Lepidoptera are moths. These range from the tiniest micro-moths that spend most of their life cycle inside leaves, to huge hawk moths that are bigger than any of our butterflies. Butterflies are simply one group on the scale from micro-moths to macro-moths.

Butterfly or moth?

To tell the difference between moths and butterflies in the UK is easier than in many parts of the world. All our butterflies are day-flying. They nearly all have small knobs on the ends of their antennae, unlike moths. They also don't have the little hooks that link a moth's front and hind wings together, called the frenulum. This makes their flight look stronger.

In a good butterfly garden in southern England, you may see 10 or more species in a day. That same garden could have over 100 different moths at night. If you want to get into learning about Lepidoptera, moths are the more interesting challenge!

This painted lady has typical butterfly antennae.

Looking at moths and butterflies

If you are going out looking for butterflies don't forget to look for day-flying moths as well. Of course most moths come out only at night, but that doesn't mean you can't see them. All you have to do is to learn how to bring them in.

Light

Many moths come to light, so can be attracted by leaving a bright light on – if you leave a bathroom window open on a warm, preferably damp summer's night, you will probably find moths inside in the morning (they are easier to find in the bathroom than among the soft furnishing of your bedroom). However, for best results you need a proper moth trap. These emit a lot of ultraviolet light as well as visible light, and this is not only especially attractive to moths but also less annoying for neighbours. There are moth enthusiasts all over the country who run moth trapping events at nature reserves. See if you can go along – you will have a great time.

Honeysuckle flowers smell sweetly at night to attract moths like the elephant hawk.

Sugar traps

You can also attract moths to sweet sticky liquids. Either soak a bit of rope in this special recipe, or paint it straight on to a tree trunk or fence post in late summer. If you are lucky, it will attract lots of moths that you can then have a look at. Some of the moths that come to sugar rarely come to light, so you could do this at the same time as putting a light trap out.

Recipe
- 300ml of liquid – preferably beer or red wine, but cola can also work
- 1kg soft brown sugar
- 0.5kg black treacle

Method
Boil all the ingredients together for five minutes until all the sugar has dissolved. Ask an adult to help. Stir all the time and then keep stirring as you let the mixture cool. When it is cold, either paint the mixture on to tree trunks, or soak lengths of cotton rope into it and hang them on trees. Keep watching as night falls.

Once your moths are in, gently encourage them to enter a small tube (yes, they will be able to breathe for hours) to get a closer look and identify them.

Day-flying moths and butterflies can also be kept in tubes, but you need to catch them first. A butterfly net has a long enough bag so that when you catch the insect with a flick of the wrist the insect is trapped in the bottom of the bag. Remember to let them go again when you've had a good look!

Binoculars

Close-focusing binoculars will be useful for watching insects, plus you can see those butterflies that rarely come down from the tree tops, such as white admirals, purple emperors and purple hairstreaks.

Look for gatekeeper butterflies resting with open wings.

Creep up slowly to see a red admiral butterfly well.

Butterflies

Summer jewels that brighten our countryside, parks and gardens.

Holly blue (about 30mm wingspan)

Identification: Pale blue both above and below, with darker tipped front wings especially in the female.

Behaviour: Flies higher than other blue butterflies.

Fact: Spring caterpillars eat holly, but the next generation later in the summer eats ivy.

Where to see it: Throughout England but rarer in other UK countries. Look around holly trees and hedges, in gardens, churchyards and hedgerows.

Don't confuse with: Common blue, which is a paler blue and has a darker underwing with more brown and black spots. There are several other blue butterflies in the UK.

Orange-tip (about 45mm wingspan)

Identification: Quite small for a white butterfly. Male has really bright orange wingtips. The female doesn't but both have beautiful green pattern under the wings.

Behaviour: One of the first butterflies to hatch from a pupa each year, so this is a real sign of spring. Watch it flying along country lanes and hedgerows and laying eggs on cuckooflower and garlic mustard.

Fact: Females taste plants with their feet to sense whether they will be suitable places for their eggs.

Where to see it: Country lanes, woodland rides and road verges throughout the UK.

Don't confuse with: Green-veined white and brimstone butterflies, which are flying around the same time, but neither has the bright orange wing tips.

Gatekeeper (about 40mm wingspan)

Identification: A golden brown butterfly of summer, with a dark spot in the centre of the upperwing.

Behaviour: Defends a small territory, often around a bramble bush, but flies to rough grassland to lay its eggs.

Fact: Only males have the brown band on the centre of the forewing.

Where to see it: Throughout England and Wales, but rarer in Scotland and Northern Ireland. Look for it in July and August where there are flowers for adults to feed on and long grass for them to lay eggs on. Field and woodland edges are good spots.

Don't confuse with: Meadow brown, which is larger, and the fritillaries, which are more ginger and patterned.

Painted lady (about 65mm wingspan)

Identification: A large, strong-flying orange butterfly with black and white wingtips and camouflaged underwings.

Behaviour: Spring sightings will be butterflies that have flown here from North Africa! These will breed on thistles or nettles before their offspring head south.

Fact: Though they can't survive our cold winter in any stage of their life cycle, this butterfly has even been found as far north as Iceland.

Where to see it: Anywhere! If there is an influx of painted ladies, they will turn up in any habitat all over the UK.

Don't confuse with: Red admiral and small tortoiseshell, which may be on the same bushes, but the former is red and black and the latter has a fringe of blue spots around its hindwing.

Micro-moths

Tiny and neglected, these little creatures are well worth a look.

Horse chestnut leafminer (5mm wingspan)

Identification: Adults are beautiful shiny gold with white stripes.

Behaviour: Caterpillars burrow into horse chestnut leaves and spend their whole time inside. A tree infected with horse chestnut leaf miners can have thousands and may look like autumn in the middle of summer.

Fact: This moth was new to science in 1984, but has now spread right across England and has been found in all other UK countries as well since first being seen in London in 2002.

Where to see it: Find horse chestnut (conker) trees and keep checking during the summer until you find the moths under leaves. There may be three broods each summer, so you should find them sooner or later.

Don't confuse with: There are 34 species in the same family! This is best identified by finding it on the right tree.

Small magpie moth (25mm wingspan)

Identification: Black and white chequer-board pattern with an orange head. Often seen in daylight.

Behaviour: Will come to lit windows or moth traps, but also easily disturbed from long grass.

Fact: The caterpillar eats stinging nettles and other weeds, which is why this moth is quite common.

Where to see it: Anywhere in England, especially in the south, but rarer in Wales and Scotland. Look along country hedgerows.

Don't confuse with: Marbled white butterfly and large magpie moth, which are both much bigger, even though this is quite large for a micro-moth!

Larger moths

The hidden gems of your garden wildlife. Also called macro-moths.

Elephant hawk (50mm wingspan)

Identification: Adult moth is a large and beautiful combination of green and pink. The caterpillar is finger length and thick, either green or brown with a soft ' spike' at the tail end.

Behaviour: Caterpillars eat rosebay willowherb and the adults visit night-scented flowers to suck nectar.

Fact: It gets its name because the caterpillar is said to look like an elephant's trunk.

Where to see it: Throughout the UK. It comes readily to light from June to September, but you may see it around honeysuckle or on buddleia by torchlight.

Don't confuse with: The small elephant hawk moth, which is even pinker, but also smaller and rarer.

Angle-shades (45mm wingspan)

Identification: The wings look as if they have been creased longways, making it look like a dry leaf. The dark triangle on the wings is always present, but the whole moth can look either green or brown.

Behaviour: This moth can have two generations in a single summer, so can be found at any time of year, even though it is most common in the summer.

Fact: The caterpillar isn't too fussy. It will eat all sorts of plants, from nettles and oak leaves to dock plants and celery.

Where to see it: Comes readily to light and sugar all over the UK, but its camouflage makes it hard to spot when resting during the day.

Don't confuse with: The small angle shades, which is smaller, darker brown, less wrinkled and less common. Watch out though, there are 2500 different moths in the UK!

Garden carpet (20mm wingspan)

Identification: Usually black and white and sitting flat on a wall. Check where the black spots are carefully. Caterpillar may be either green or brown.

Behaviour: Caterpillars move in a looping movement rather than wriggling (imagine walking on all fours with your hands and feet tied!) Easily disturbed from garden plants.

Fact: Garden carpet moths are in the geometer family. This means 'ground measuring' and reflects the movement of the caterpillars.

Where to see it: As the name suggest, this is a common moth in gardens. It can be found throughout the summer all over the UK, coming to light or sugar.

Don't confuse with: Many similar species of geometer, including over 160 close relatives.

Buff arches (35-40mm wingspan)

Identification: Delicate combination of browns and greys, with fantastic wavy lines near the end of the wings make this one of our prettiest moths, especially seen under a hand lens.

Behaviour: The caterpillar eats bramble leaves and the adult moth comes to light and sugar in woodland and gardens.

Fact: These moths can hear bats coming and drop out of the sky to avoid being eaten.

Where to see it: Found throughout England, Wales and Northern Ireland, but rare in Scotland.

Don't confuse with: There are 15 species in this family. The whole family also looks similar to an even bigger family called the noctuids.

Grasshoppers and crickets

Long-legged jumpers that sing in the late summer.

Field grasshopper (18-24mm long)

Identification: Can be green or brown, but always with long, strong back legs and antennae that are shorter than its body.

Behaviour: Despite being best known for jumping, these can be quite strong flyers. You may see them sunning on walls or paths, but you can also hear their 'chirp chirp chirp' call.

Fact: Grasshoppers have ears on their back ends.

Where to see it: In summer and autumn in long grass or nearby paths and walls in the sun.

Don't confuse with: 11 different grasshoppers live in the UK.

Roesel's bush-cricket (15-25mm long)

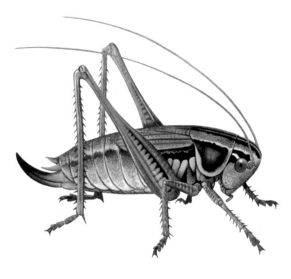

Identification: Usually brown and with pale spots along its side, just behind a big pale U-shaped mark. Very long antennae.

Behaviour: Sings loudly from long grass from June to September. The song is a long, continuous high-pitched hiss, above the hearing of many adults.

Fact: It used to live in southern England, but is rapidly spreading north and west.

Where to see it: In long grass, meadows and unkempt road verges right across lowland England and surely soon in the rest of the UK.

Don't confuse with: The very long antennae and, on females, the long curved egg-laying tube (it's not a stinger) help tell bush crickets from grasshoppers, but there are 10 species in the UK.

Ants, wasps and bees

Narrow-waisted insects that reveal the three-part body plan: head, thorax and abdomen.

Southern wood ant (8mm long)

Identification: This is a very big, dark red-brown ant that lives in huge colonies in open pine woods.

Behaviour: You can watch ants for days as they work together for the sake of their colony, which is a huge heap of pine needles.

Fact: A big wood ant colony can collect and bring back over 60,000 food items every day.

Where to see it: In open woodland in southern England and Wales. Look for big heaps (several buckets full) of pine needles crawling with ants, or follow trails of ants that you see crossing woodland tracks.

Don't confuse with: Garden ants. The three species of wood ants in the UK are much larger.

Wood wasp (4cm long)

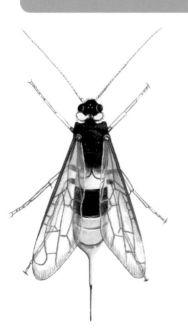

Identification: Big, fierce-looking, but completely harmless black and yellow wasp. Female has a long spike sticking out of its back end. It's not a sting; it's an egg-laying tube.

Behaviour: Uses its long egg-laying tube (called an ovipositor) to lay its eggs deep inside rotting wood. The grub eats the wood inside until it hatches out two years later.

Fact: The female may take as long as 15 minutes to drill a hole through the bark of a tree to lay her egg in the hard wood beneath.

Where to see it: Never common, but in woods and gardens throughout the UK. Occasionally hatches from timber in houses so may be seen against the window – be brave and let it out!

Don't confuse with: Hornets, which are fatter, more like huge browner wasps. There are perhaps 150 different sawflies in the UK, but this is the biggest.

Ruby-tailed jewel wasp (12mm long)

Identification: Bright metallic turquoise head and body and shiny red tail. This is smaller than garden wasps and usually seen on its own.

Behaviour: Tracks down other solitary wasps and lays its eggs in their nests where it will eat their larvae.

Fact: Jewel wasps are usually noticed only in bright sunshine and are sometimes called cuckoo wasps. They don't sting.

Where to see it: On heathlands and in gardens throughout the UK. Look for other solitary wasps and bees and you may see this nearby, perhaps feeding on pollen in flowers.

Don't confuse with: There are other similar species, but this is the most commonly seen.

Buff-tailed bumblebee (1.5-2.5cm long)

Identification: One of the classic hairy, black and yellow bumblebees. Queens are biggest and have buff tails. The smaller workers come out later in the year. They have white tails.

Behaviour: Queens emerge first in the spring and build a small nest which may contain up to 300 bees by late summer.

Where to see it: In gardens, parks, hedgerows and flower meadows across the UK, and earlier in the spring than many species.

Don't confuse with: White-tailed bumblebee, which is a bit smaller and even the queen has a white tail. There are around 25 bumblebee species in the UK and far more lone mining bees.

Flies

Flies have just two main flight wings whereas bees, butterflies and moths have four.

Flesh-fly (15mm long)

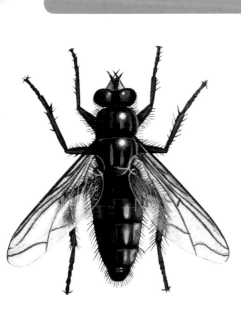

Identification: Quite large and harmless flies, usually with red eyes and with pale stripes or a chequer-board pattern running along the body.

Behaviour: Females lay their eggs or living maggots on dead and rotting animals. Some even lay eggs in open wounds on living animals! The adult flies suck up all sorts of sugary and meaty liquids.

Fact: Their life cycle is so predictable that forensic scientists can tell when a dead body died by examining the flesh-flies living on them.

Where to see it: Found across the UK, but rarely indoors. You will see plenty of them on any dead animal you come across.

Don't confuse with: Picture-wing and horse flies look similar but often have multi-coloured eyes – and they bite!

Greater bee-fly (14-18mm long)

Identification: Brown and furry like a small bumblebee, but with a long proboscis sticking out of the front of its face.

Behaviour: Hovers perfectly still in mid-air above woodland glades and tracks, and visits spring flowers such as primroses to take nectar.

Fact: Not only does this look like a bee, but its young eat bees. The mother bee-fly flicks her eggs towards the entrance holes of solitary bees. When the maggots hatch out, they crawl into the bee's home and start eating its larvae!

Where to see it: Found across the UK and usually seen from March to May.

Don't confuse with: Its long legs, sticky-out proboscis and hovering flight help to tell this apart from the bees.

St Mark's fly (12-14mm long)

Identification: Males are slow-moving, hairy black flies with long dangly legs that dance at around head height in the spring. The females are a little larger and with smaller eyes. They will be perched on leaves nearby watching.

Behaviour: Adult males live for around a week, during which time they are completely focused on finding mates. The females will mate, lay eggs underground and then die. For most of the year, this fly exists only as wriggling larvae.

Fact: The fly is named after its supposed hatching date. St Mark's Day is 25 April.

Where to see it: Over rough grassland, woodland rides and hedgerows across the UK.

Don't confuse with: This is one of 20 species in the same family, and there are over 7,000 flies in the UK, but this is the one you are most likely to notice.

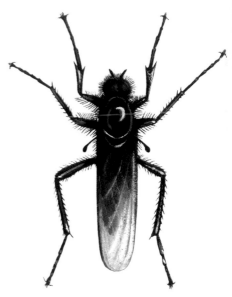

Marmalade hoverfly (10mm)

Identification: Much smaller than wasps, with orange and black bands across its abdomen and fainter stripes along its thorax. Hovers a lot, but also visits garden flowers.

Behaviour: The larvae eat aphids, but the adults visit flowers for nectar and pollen. Males can be seen hovering in sunny spots. They will be defending a territory near an aphid colony.

Fact: The UK sometimes get huge influxes of these from abroad. These tiny insects can fly here from across the sea!

Where to see it: Across the UK in gardens, woodlands and hedgerows. Expect greater numbers after spring and late summer migrations.

Don't confuse with: Wasps! Hoverflies don't sting and there are over 250 species in the UK.

Bugs

In America, all minibeasts are known as bugs, but true bugs all have piercing mouthparts to suck up food.

Hawthorn shield bug (17mm long)

Identification: Yes, shield bugs are shaped like shields! This one is green and brown with dull red eyes.

Behaviour: Uses its mouthparts like a straw to suck juices from hawthorn berries and leaves, but often remains well hidden and slow moving.

Fact: These bugs are sometimes called stink bugs. Now see if you can find one to discover why!

Where to see it: Hawthorn bushes and even oak trees throughout the UK have these camouflaged insects hiding in them. You will most likely see one that has been surprised out in the open.

Don't confuse with: The shape will help you identify shield bugs but there are about 45 species in the UK.

Rhododendron leafhopper (11mm long)

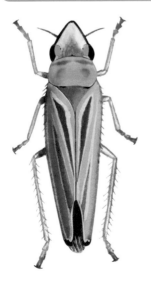

Identification: The scarlet stripes on a green background make this one of our most recognisable leafhoppers.

Behaviour: Sucks sap from within rhododendron leaves. Quite approachable, but will hop away with a click of its back legs if you get too close.

Fact: This is one of the very few insects that eat rhododendron.

Where to see it: Look in late summer on rhododendron leaves, mainly in southern England.

Don't confuse with: The shape makes this clearly a leafhopper, but if you find one of a different colour beware. There are over 400 other species to choose from!

Stilt bug (12-18mm long)

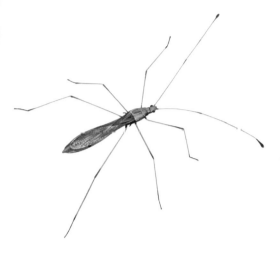

Identification: All 100 or so species have very long legs and long antennae. They are often camouflaged against the leaves they live on, being usually plain green, brown or grey.

Behaviour: They walk slowly along the plant leaves and stems, and often freeze if they think they have been spotted.

Fact: Although stilt bugs eat plant juices, they have relatives, such as the assassin bugs, that hunt other insects and suck them dry!

Where to see them: You can find stilt bugs in many different habitats, but one of the easiest ways is to go tree-beating.

Don't confuse with: Other than the other 99 stilt bugs, don't mistake this for a spider – it only has six legs.

Pond skater (12-15mm long)

Identification: A grey bug scooting over a pond surface, with its body raised up on long legs will be a pond skater.

Behaviour: Often waits at the edges of the pond, detecting the vibrations of a dying insect that has fallen in. Then it uses its middle legs to skate out, pierce the hapless victim with its beak and suck it dry. Lovely!

Fact: Pond skaters have water-repellent hairs on their feet to help them glide on the water's surface tension.

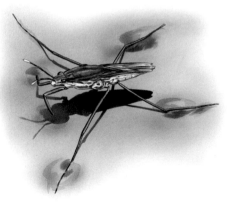

Where to see them: Any pond will have pond skaters, but quieter ones without fish will be best. You can see these insects on mild days, even late into the autumn and early in spring.

Don't confuse with: There are seven similar species in the UK, along with water-measurers. These move much more slowly and look gangly compared with pond skaters.

Beetles

One of the most interesting and diverse groups of insects, but tricky to identify.

Click beetle (9-13mm long)

Identification: A long, slim beetle, pale brown with its head and thorax sunken. Close up, its antennae are jointed.

Behaviour: The larvae are grubs that live under the bark of all sorts of trees. Adults can be found feeding on pollen in garden flowers and on trees.

Fact: If you hold one, it may flex its body quickly to right itself or escape. This is the 'click' that gives these beetles their name.

Where to see it: Through the UK, in the summer on garden flowers and in woodlands, often in your sheet after tree-beating.

Don't confuse with: There are 73 different click beetles in the UK, mostly plain browns or black.

Devil's coach-horse (25-30mm)

Identification: Large, flexible black beetle, a bit like a giant earwig.

Behaviour: Voracious predator that isn't afraid to turn on people and give them a nip, but more usually it arches its tail in threat, perhaps imitating a scorpion.

Fact: When threatened, it can release a foul-smelling white fluid that may stop small mammals attacking it.

Where to see it: It usually hides under logs or stones in the daytime and comes out to hunt at night. You are most likely to see one running across a footpath or perhaps in a pitfall trap – when it may have eaten anything else that fell into the same trap.

Don't confuse with: This is one of around 1,000 rove beetles in the UK, but its size marks it out. Earwigs are much smaller and brown.

Common red soldier beetle (12-15mm long)

Identification: A slim mainly dull orange beetle with a black tail end. Often seen in pairs.

Behaviour: The larvae spend most of their time on the ground hunting for smaller creatures to eat. The adults survive for only a few weeks and spend much of their time mating.

Fact: Many children call these bloodsuckers, but soldier beetles are completely harmless to humans.

Where to see it: Across the UK, in parks, gardens, meadows and woodland rides.

Don't confuse with: There are around 40 different soldier beetles in the UK.

Cockchafer (up to 30mm long)

Identification: Large, blundering brown summer beetle, with whirring flight and fantastic branched antennae.

Behaviour: Flies from dusk in May and June and can be very common in some places. If one lands on your clothing, it can grip surprisingly strongly, but they are harmless and generally slow-moving.

Fact: Cockchafer grubs can live in the soil for up to four years before hatching as adults.

Where to see it: Across the UK, in gardens, parks and woodland edges. The adults favour broad-leaved trees.

Don't confuse with: Other chafers, which are smaller or more brightly coloured, but we have around 4,000 beetles in the UK.

Other insects

We can't cover all the 20,000 insects in the UK, but here are a couple of lovely oddities.

Silverfish (15-20mm)

Identification: Imagine a shiny, fast moving cross between a centipede and a woodlouse and you have a silverfish. No wings, three tails and long antennae help.

Behaviour: They come out at night and pick up leftovers from crumbs and dead insects to glue and cardboard.

Fact: Silverfish have been around since the time of the dinosaurs.

Where to see it: Usually indoors on hard surfaces. They prefer damp and unheated homes. Look in old bathrooms or under your kitchen sink, or in old church corners.

Don't confuse with: Marine bristletails, found under seaweedy rocks above the high-water mark on beaches right around our coasts. They are much larger.

Moorhen flea (2mm long)

Identification: Fleas are all small, slippery, wingless and shiny with huge back legs. They are flattened so that they can run through fur and feathers with ease.

Behaviour: They bite to drink blood as food and mostly crawl slowly along. The famous flea jump is for getting from one host animal or its nest to another.

Fact: Moorhen fleas tend to stay on the bird (not just moorhens!) but may also live in old nests. If you find a freshly dead bird, its fleas will be trying to escape as the body cools down.

Where to see it: Different creatures have different sorts of flea. For bird fleas this often depends on the sort of nest the bird makes.

Don't confuse with: If you can keep them still, types of fleas look different under a magnifying glass. They may be different colours and sizes and some have arched backs where others have rounded backs.

Other minibeasts – spiders

Eight legs, eight eyes, poison fangs and neither wings nor antennae – spiders are perfect little hunters. They don't all spin webs.

Zebra spider (5-7mm)

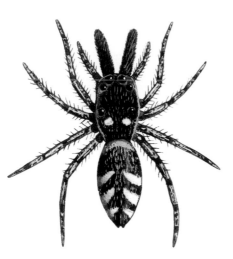

Identification: Black-and-white striped, with two bigger forward-facing eyes to help it judge its distance from its prey.

Behaviour: Creeps up on prey its own size in a jerky fashion, then jumps on the insect. If you get too close, it will probably turn to have a look at you – don't worry, it's harmless to people.

Fact: Jumping spiders fix themselves a safety line of silk before they jump – so they can climb back up if they miss their target.

Where to see it: Window frames, sunny walls and garden fences in the summer are easiest, but you can also find them stalking insects on tree trunks.

Don't confuse with: There are other jumping spiders, but this one is quite distinctive.

Fen raft spider (up to 70mm leg span)

Identification: Our biggest spider. Chocolate brown with a pale cream stripe along its side. As with other spiders, the female is much bigger than the male.

Behaviour: Waits at the edge of ponds with its front legs on the water surface. When it feels a ripple, it rushes out across the water surface to grab its prey. But also hunts by swimming under water.

Fact: Despite being big enough to catch small fish, this spider was only first noticed in Britain in the 1950s.

Where to see it: This spider lives in ponds in bogs and reedbed pools but in only a few places nowadays. Conservationists are breeding them to release in new areas to help the species survive.

Don't confuse with: The common house spider is the huge hairy beast that runs across your floor, but there are 600 other types of spider in the UK.

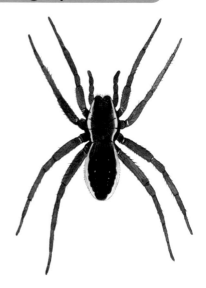

Daddy long-legs spider

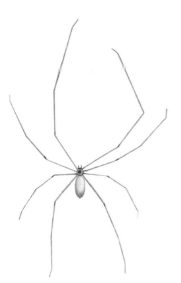

Identification: Very long thin legs that make it look more like a daddy long legs than a normal spider.

Behaviour: Hangs upside-down in a rather feeble web in the corner of a room, waiting to go hunting at night. If you disturb it, the spider will vibrate its web so quickly that it becomes almost invisible.

Fact: The long legs of this spider help keep dangerous prey, such as other spiders, at arm's length while it is bundling them up in silk.

Where to see it: Look in the high corners of rooms, especially in southern Britain. Even though this is a wild animal, you won't find one outdoors because it can't cope with the cold.

Don't confuse with: Real daddy long-legs have two wings and six legs.

Woodlouse spider

Identification: The pale reddish brown body and huge fangs make this unmistakeable. It is not as quick moving as many of our spiders so you have plenty of time to get a closer look.

Behaviour: During the day, this spider stays under dry stones in a silk bed, but comes out at night to hunt its favourite prey – woodlice.

Fact: Most of our spiders don't have jaws strong enough to bite people, but this one does because it is adapted for crunching through woodlice.

Where to see it: They sometimes come into houses, but you are more likely to find one under a brick in your garden.

Don't confuse with: One other similar species, but it is much rarer.

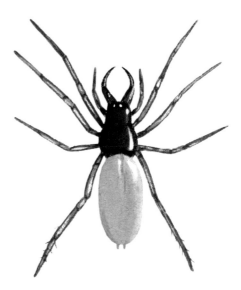

Crustaceans

There are so many different types of crustacean that ways to look at one won't help much when you look at another. What works for studying woodlice (such as looking under stones in your garden) won't work for looking at lobsters in the sea!

However, there are similarities that may help. Crustaceans have 10 jointed legs, and they are likely to want to get away before you can study them. In general, they are shy, live in holes and most eat anything they can catch. This means that you will have to go looking in holes, often at night and that you can sometimes tempt them out with tasty titbits.

The obvious example here is crabbing. To catch crabs and have a look at them, you need a fishing line with a bit of bait on the end – usually meat or fish – and then somewhere that crabs live. Piers and rockpools are good places. To avoid hurting the crab, rather than attach your bait with a hook, you could tie it on, perhaps in a little mesh bag – such as an emptied teabag. The crabs will be so keen that you can haul them up still clinging on to their food!

Woodlice

Most crustaceans, including crabs, lobsters, prawns and barnacles are marine creatures, but woodlice live on the land. You may even find them indoors, where they come out at night to look for scraps. However, you are more likely to find them under plant pots in a greenhouse, in the shed or under logs and stones.

There are 40 species of woodlice in the UK, but some of them are very rare. The more common ones are easy to study in an old fish tank. Keep them for a few days and find out where they prefer to live. Will they go to the damp or dry spots?

Woodlice have lots of old country names including cheesy bug, rolypoly and chuggypig!

Most crustaceans live in water. There may be over 70,000 different types worldwide.

Acorn barnacle (up to 15mm across)

Identification: Acorn barnacles are the small white or pale brown shell-like cones that cling to seashore rocks and shellfish, and that stop you slipping into the waves.

Behaviour: Acorn barnacles spend their whole adult lives clinging to the same rock or shell. They open their shells and wave their feet out of the top to look for food.

Fact: Baby barnacles drift through the sea as part of the plankton, but once they choose a surface to settle on, they stick there for life.

Where to see it: On rocks, sea defences and on the backs of crabs and shells all around the coast in the intertidal zone.

Don't confuse with: The diamond-shaped opening (as opposed to oval or round) helps to set this apart from other species.

Water flea (less than 2mm across)

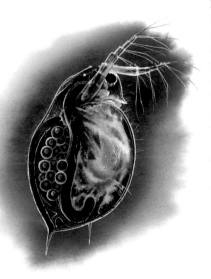

Identification: The tiniest creatures that you are likely to be able to see. Water fleas are mostly see-through, and move through the water in a skipping motion.

Behaviour: Skips through the water in search of even tinier things to eat, such as bacteria and tiny plants.

Fact: Water fleas are the first animals on many food chains. Without water fleas there would be no otters or kingfishers.

Where to see it: Hold a glass of pond or river water up to the light, and look for little jumpers. You will need a microscope to have a proper look.

Don't confuse with: There are around 80 different types of water flea in the UK, but this is among the most common. Fish shops sometimes sell bags of giant water fleas (although they are still very small!) as fish food.

Sea slater (up to 30mm long)

Identification: Like a giant grey or green woodlouse.

Behaviour: Stays hidden in a crack or under rocks and seaweeds on rocky shores during the day. Comes out at night to find all sorts of things to eat.

Fact: Sea slaters can live for up to three years.

Where to see it: On the upper shore right around our coast. Look under seaweed on the strand line. You will often find quite a lot together.

Don't confuse with: Other woodlice, which are much smaller and don't live on the seashore.

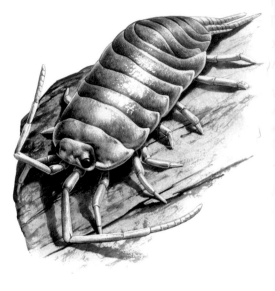

Lobster (up to 50cm long)

Identification: Huge claws, bluish shell, 10 pairs of legs and a flattened body. This is a sea species. Crayfish in some of our lakes and rivers have similar body plans but are much smaller.

Behaviour: Lobsters live in holes in rocks in shallow seas and come out to catch fish and other creatures, dead or alive.

Fact: Wild lobsters can live for more than 15 years, as long as they aren't caught by people.

Where to see it: Lobsters live below the low tide line, so you are most likely to see one as part of a fishing boat's catch.

Don't confuse with: There is only one species of lobster in UK seas, and its shape should stop you confusing it with anything else.

Molluscs

Nearly a quarter of all known sea creatures are molluscs. There are plenty living on land and in freshwater as well. They range from octopuses and giant squids, to limpets, oysters, slugs and snails. It can be quite hard to decide what is and isn't a mollusc!

Most have shells, but not all. Most eat plants, but not all. And most prefer damp or wet places to live, but again, not all. Most are slow moving by human standards, especially the land molluscs, but others, such as cuttlefish, are fast moving. Some barely see the world at all through tiny eyes, but others have eyes that are every bit as good as our own.

Looking at molluscs

Molluscs can be studied alive or dead. By dead, I mean by collecting seashells or investigating whether particular colours of snail shell are more common on song thrush anvils than others.

Watching living land molluscs and even many of those at the seaside is all about knowing where to look. Start with damp places – under logs and stones, in ponds or rockpools.

When you find a snail or slug that has curled up and hidden away from the drying sun, you can often coax it out to get a decent look by splashing it with fresh water (or seawater for molluscs you find on the beach). Give it a little time to detect the water and the creature may come out to see what's going on.

Find mussels below the high water line at the seaside.

Leopard slug (up to 20cm long)

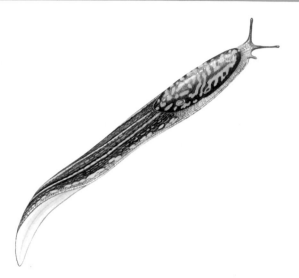

Identification: A huge and attractive slug with bold black and white stripes on the tail and leopard spotting on its back.

Behaviour: These slugs mate for hours while hanging from a sticky rope that they make.

Fact: This is one of the biggest slugs in the world!

Where to see it: Always near humans, perhaps in a damp cellar or wet corner of an outhouse where it can eat mouldy wood.

Don't confuse with: There are around 30 different slugs in the UK, but this is the biggest you are likely to see.

Banded snail (shell up to 20mm tall)

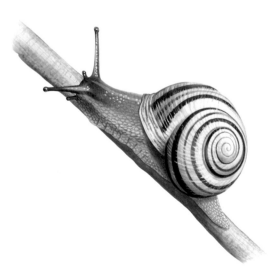

Identification: A medium-sized snail with lovely swirls of brown, cream, white or yellow, spiralling round the shell.

Behaviour: Only active in the spring and summer. They hibernate all winter.

Fact: These snails' patterns help them avoid being seen by their arch enemy, the song thrush.

Where to see them: Very common in grassland throughout the UK.

Don't confuse with: There are two similar species, one with a pale lip to the shell and one with a dark lip.

Shellfish

Shells provide protection for these seaside molluscs.

Blue-rayed limpet (up to 15mm across)

Identification: Oval, amber coloured but see-through shell with lines of bright electric blue spots.

Behaviour: Blue-rayed limpets cling to and graze the seaweed just below the low-water mark, especially on rough coasts.

Fact: You find the biggest and oldest blue-rayed limpets near to the holdfast, where the seaweed clings on to its rock.

Where to see it: Look on the huge oarweed seaweed at the lowest of tides, either in rockpools or by snorkelling over them. They can sometimes be found still clinging to seaweed that's been washed up on the beach after a storm.

Don't confuse with: The other limpets, which are much larger, live higher up the beach and don't have the electric blue bling!

Edible or blue mussel (up to 10cm long)

Identification: Purple, blue, black or sometimes brown, with two shells that mirror one another. Usually in clumps of hundreds together.

Behaviour: Mussels are filter feeders. This means they suck sea water in, filter out tiny particles to eat and then squirt the remaining water out again. That's why you never see open mussels above the water line.

Fact: Mussels can work together to tie down predatory whelks with strong threads that they grow.

Where to see it: Mussels occur around all our coasts. The easiest places to see them are stuck on the wooden posts of piers and harbours – or at your local supermarket fish counter.

Don't confuse with: This is the only bivalve – two-shelled animal – of this size and colour.

Other animals

We can't cover everything in the one small book, but we couldn't leave these out!

Centipede (up to 5cm long)

Identification: Usually red or brown with a single pair of legs for each segment. Looks like it has been flattened.

Behaviour: Lives under logs and stones, but may come out at night. A keen hunter of smaller creatures.

Fact: Despite centipede meaning 100 feet, ours rarely have more than 30.

Where to see it: Under stones and logs throughout the UK.

Don't confuse with: Millipedes, which have two pairs of legs per body segment and look much rounder when seen head-on.

Medicinal leech (up to 20cm long)

Identification: A big, stretchy, dark, worm-like creature, often with green or orange stripes running down it.

Behaviour: Feeds by attaching itself to an animal and sucking blood. Their slinky movement is fantastic.

Fact: Doctors used to bleed people with leeches to try to remove blood poisons. It didn't work.

Where to see it: They are now quite rare, but found throughout Britain in muddy ponds.

Don't confuse with: Many much smaller leeches, which live in ponds.

Soil mites (microscopic – under 1mm long)

Identification: Soil mites are tiny and often white. You will need a good hand lens or microscope to see one well. When you do so, it will probably have a rounded body and eight tiny little legs.

Behaviour: They spend their time eating even tinier creatures, such as soil bacteria, and trying not to be eaten themselves.

Fact: If you lie down on the grass, you will have more soil mites beneath you than there are people on the planet!

Where to see it: Under a microscope near you – all soil has mites.

Don't confuse with: Soil mites are slow moving, unlike the primitive bouncing springtail insects that you may also see in soil.

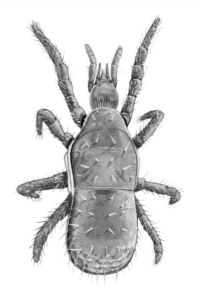

Dead-man's fingers (up to 250mm tall)

Identification: A soft coral that looks like it has fingers sticking out of the colony. It is often white, but may be brown or orange.

Behaviour: It sticks its tentacles out into the strong current to catch tiny animals that are swept past.

Fact: Colonies of dead man's fingers are usually either all male or all female, but all the colonies in an area release their eggs together.

Where to see it: At the very low-water line down to 100m below water, all around our coasts.

Don't confuse with: Other soft corals and sponges.

Common brittle star (up to 50mm across)

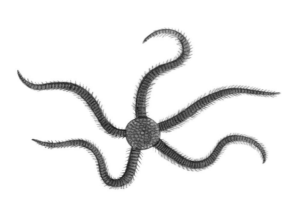

Identification: Round grey or brown body with five bristly legs that look as though they have been stuck on.

Behaviour: Usually seen moving very slowly in a rocky or sandy tidal pool, when it will be feeding on tiny creatures or anything else that drifts by.

Fact: Brittle stars are really brittle and their arms can snap off very easily. But they can grow new ones.

Where to see it: Often overlooked, but you can find these in tidal pools right around the UK's coasts. Sometimes they bury themselves just under the sandy bottom.

Don't confuse with: There are many different brittle stars in our seas, but they all have the same body shape. Other starfish look more at one with their legs.

Sea orange sponge (up to 40cm across)

Identification: Usually orange or red, but sometimes duller brown when growing deeper in the sea. It can be a range of shapes and always has a few obvious holes in it.

Behaviour: Sponges don't move much, so if you see one of these attached to a rock don't expect it to walk off. It spends its life filtering tiny bits of food from the sea.

Fact: Despite looking more like a fungus, a sponge is a colony of tiny animals. It is said that if you put one through a blender it will re-form and carry on living, but please don't try this!

Where to see them: Low down on the shore or from harbour walls all around our coasts.

Don't confuse with: There are over 160 sponges in the UK and many of them look very different dead out of the water compared with being alive. Several are orange.

Worms and anemones

Soft-bodied, but no less successful for the lack of bones or a shell.

Earthworm (up to 25cm long)

Identification: Pinky grey worm, with paler brownish saddle near the head end – that's the end at the front when the worm is travelling along.

Behaviour: This worm digs a burrow, but comes to the surface to find dead leaves and even dead insects to drag into its home to eat.

Fact: Earthworms can live for at least six years if they don't get eaten by a robin or hedgehog.

Where to see it: This is the most common worm in lawns and is the one you are most likely to see on a pavement after rain.

Don't confuse with: There may be 3,000 different types of worms worldwide, but no one is quite sure how many live in the UK.

Strawberry sea-anemone (75mm across)

Identification: Above water, it looks like a big, green-flecked strawberry. Underwater, it spreads its ring of stinging tentacles.

Behaviour: Spends low tide just above the water under a ledge in a rockpool, spreading its tentacles when the water rises to cover it. The tentacles have stinging tips to help the anemone catch small swimming creatures to eat.

Fact: Sea anemones stick on to the rock so hard that you would hurt one trying to take it off – so please don't.

Where to see it: Low down on rocky shores in southern England.

Don't confuse with: Beadlet anemone, which is smaller, and doesn't have the green spots, but it is found around all our coasts.

Parasites

These plants and animals spend their whole lives living on or in another life form.

Tapeworm (up to 30m long, but can be smaller)

Identification: Adult tapeworms are usually white and their bodies are made up of many identical segments.

Behaviour: Adults live in the gut of their main host – bird, mammal, fish, amphibian, reptile or fish. They lay eggs in the animal's poo. These hatch and live in another creature until it is eaten by one of the main hosts, where it grows to be another adult.

Fact: Like other parasites, tapeworms rarely kill their host – after all, the host is their lifeline.

Where to see it: You probably never will unless your pet has one – they stay hidden inside other animals.

Don't confuse with: There are over 1,000 types of tapeworms and plenty of other parasites, such as the roundworms that are smooth and lack the body segments.

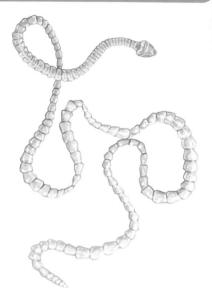

Greater dodder (stems up to 1m long)

Identification: Long, thin, red stems twining around nettle or thistle plants, but with no obvious leaves. White or pink flowers.

Behaviour: When its seeds hatch, dodder sniffs out a plant to grow towards, then attaches itself to the host and steals all its food.

Fact: In some places this parasitic plant used to be known as 'devil's guts'. Lovely!

Where to see it: Mainly in southern and eastern England, in nettlebeds, on hedgerows and river banks.

Don't confuse with: Other dodder species, which live in drier places. The lack of leaves and yellow, orange or green stems should help you be sure that you are seeing dodder.

246

Trees

Trees are big, easy to find and don't run away, but that doesn't make them dull or easy to identify. There is a lot to tree watching, and that's before you even start to look at what lives in them.

Looking at trees

There are five things to look for when identifying a tree, but you don't have to see them all every time.

1. Its overall size and shape – often different in summer and winter. Look for the angle of branches coming from the main trunk and how straight they are. Do this from a distance.

2. Bark and buds – is the bark smooth, deeply lined, or cracked and peeling? Is it grey or reddish brown, or even silver? And look closely at the buds, especially in winter. Their colour will help, and you may also be able to work out how the leaves are going to grow. You will be doing this from close up – the tree won't escape.

3. The size and shape of the leaves – check whether the edges are smooth or toothed, whether the whole leaf is corrugated or smooth and how big it is. Do the leaves grow in bunches or is each one very separate? Beware leaves under a tree that may have blown in from elsewhere.

4. Flowers – Some trees have very obvious spring flowers, such as horse chestnuts (conker trees). Others have little green flowers. The showy ones need to attract insects. The others have pollen that blows in the wind.

5. Fruits and nuts – From conkers to crab apples or beech nuts to pine cones, a tree's seeds are distinctive, but often don't last long – especially if a squirrel gets there first.

Look for acorns on oak trees in autumn.

How tall and how old?

Two things you may want to know about any trees you find are: how tall is it and how old is it?

How tall?

Walk away from the tree and stop. Now bend over and look back at the tree through your legs.

If you can't see the top of the tree, walk on a bit farther and try again.

When you can just see the very top of the tree through your legs, stand up.

Turn around and count the number of big paces from you to the tree, and then do the maths.

Number of paces X length of each pace in metres = height of the tree. Most people's paces are around a metre long.

The distinctive white peeling bark of silver birch will help you identify it.

How old?

Different types of tree grow at different speeds. Silver birch trees, for example, grow much quicker than yew trees. Even the same sort of trees may grow differently, depending on the soil, the rainfall and how much light they get and even whether they have been regularly pruned by people or grazing animals. However, there is an easy way to get a rough idea of how old a living tree is:

Measure all the way around the trunk of the tree about 1.3m above the ground (above the broadest part where the tree's roots spread into the ground).

Multiply this number in centimetres by 0.4 to get a rough age in years.

If you find a fresh tree stump, see if you can count the tree rings. You should find one per year that the tree grew, but they can be hard to see.

Conifer trees

Pine, fir and other conifer trees all have thin needle-like leaves. Most keep their leaves all year round.

Yew (up to 20m tall)

Identification: Dense, dark and bushy, with bright red fruit-like cones called arils. Thin leaves arranged in two flattened rows of spirals. Thin, flaky, reddish brown bark.

Fact: This tree can live for thousands of years. Most parts are poisonous to people.

Uses: Yew wood was used to make longbows in the middle ages. All parts of the tree are used in medicines, but it has also been used as a poison.

Where to see it: You will find this tree in old churchyards, and it is also used in hedges in country houses. It is hard to find in the wild now because so many were used to make bows.

Don't confuse with: Juniper, which is smaller with blue berries; Leyland cypress, which is the common, often unruly bushy tree of many garden hedges.

Scots Pine (up to 40m tall)

Identification: Long, bare straight trunk and a mass of needles on top. The needles are blue-green and grow in pairs. The cones start out red, before turning green and then brown in the two years they take to mature.

Fact: Scotland's national tree. Ancient Scots pine forests are among our most important wildlife habitats.

Uses: This tree is planted a lot for its timber and for wood pulp for making paper – perhaps even this book.

Where to see it: The Highlands in Scotland still have some native pine forest with these trees, but you can also see them planted in many places, especially where the soil is poor and sandy.

Don't confuse with: Other conifers such as Norway spruce and Douglas fir, which have a pyramidal, Christmas-tree shape.

Deciduous trees

They lose their leaves in winter as a way to save water.

Wild cherry (up to around 30m tall)

Identification: Straight trunk with dark red-brown smooth bark that flakes. Masses of white flowers come out at the same time as the leaves in early spring. Look for cherries in the summer.

Fact: Cherry trees produce cherries that birds and animals then eat. The cherry stone passes through the animal's gut. The poo acts as fertiliser for the seedling.

Uses: Cherry wood is very hard, so is a prized wood for craft workers. But did you know that cuts in cherry bark will leak a healing goo that can be used as chewing gum?

Where to see it: Throughout the UK, especially on chalky soils, and commonly on the edges of woodlands or in hedgerows because it likes more light than the centre of a wood can provide.

Don't confuse with: Smaller, pink-flowered Japanese cherries are commonly planted along suburban roadsides.

Goat willow (up to 12m tall)

Identification: One of the pussy willows, so called because of its furry-looking female flowers. Often has many stems.

Fact: Male and female trees are separate, which is why you will only see pussy willow catkins on half the trees. The wind blows the pollen between the trees, but bees also go mad for it.

Uses: Willow bark contains the active chemical in aspirin.

Where to see them: Damp open woodlands and along the banks of slow-moving rivers and canals.

Don't confuse with: There are many similar willows and hybrids which makes them very hard to identify, but the leaves and catkins will get you as far as willow tree.

Wildflowers

You can find wildflowers from early spring right through to late autumn, and even in the winter in southerly sheltered places. However, April to August is the main time to see them. Some of the earliest flowers are on woodland floors, where they aim to catch the sun and visiting insects before the tree leaves block out the light.

In May and June, hedgerows and flower meadows are at their peak, especially in the south. Later, in July and August, and farther north, the flowers of the uplands and lowland heaths bloom. The hills turn purple with heather.

There are a few flowers that only come out in autumn. This may be reflected in their names, such as the autumn gentian.

Flowers are there for one purpose: to help the plant reproduce itself. The flowers themselves may be adapted to attract butterflies, moths, bees or other flying insects, or they may be simply open to the wind.

It is usually much easier to identify the plant when it is flowering, but a few species, such as cuckoo pint, have such distinctive berries that many people notice them only in the autumn.

Primroses are much less common than they used to be.

Watching wildflowers

To study wildflowers you need patience – waiting for them to flower or to open is half the battle. Once they have done so, you will want to get a close look, so a hand lens is useful. These days, most people prefer to record their flowers by photographing them, but there is a long tradition of painting and preserving wildflowers.

Painting flowers

Botanical artists have a reputation for exactness, and a good botanical illustration can usually say more about the plant than an average photograph. However, it takes time and almost always means picking the flower and bringing it indoors. Unless you have permission, please leave wildflowers for everyone to enjoy.

Pressing flowers

Preserving flowers is usually done by pressing them. Freshly picked flowers are arranged on tissue paper and placed between two boards. They are then squashed for weeks under a heavy weight or by screwing the boards down in a proper flower press. The result usually preserves the form of the flower, but the colours tend to fade, so this technique is best combined with painting or photography.

Growing flowers

Collecting and drying the seeds of wildflowers means that you can grow them at home, especially if they are local, so the soil is similar. Collect seed pods in paper envelopes to stop the seed rotting, and store them in a shed or unheated place (away from house mice!). Plant them in the spring.

Willowherb seeds are fluffy and float on the wind to find new homes.

Wildflowers of wetlands

Wetland flowers are often quite tall because they can get all the water they need to grow.

Flag iris (up to 1.5m tall)

Identification: Very tall flower spike with a bright yellow, floppy-looking flower that has three big drooping petals and three more horizontal ones. Often grows in a clump.

Fact: Big clumps, or stands, of irises that have spread by rhizomes grow in damp corners, wetland and ponds, but the flowers also produce seeds that float away and grow into new plants when they settle.

Uses: The flowers, underground rhizomes and stems of flag irises have been used to create dyes for fabrics. Depending how they are treated, it can make yellow, green, brown or even black dyes.

Where to see it: In ditches, ponds and reedbeds throughout the UK, but the biggest iris beds are perhaps in western Scotland.

Don't confuse with: Stinking iris, which is our only other native iris and is bluey-grey. You may also encounter other species that have escaped from gardens.

Meadowsweet (up to 1.5m tall)

Identification: Paired crinkly leaves, each with three lobes on spindly, sometimes reddish stems give way to frothy white clumps of flowers that smell very sweet.

Fact: Thick mats of meadowsweet in damp meadows get full of insects.

Uses: The plant contains the chemical that aspirin is made from, and because it smells so sweet was sometimes strewn around indoors to mask dodgy smells.

Where to see it: In damp meadows, along stream banks and in damp woodland rides across the UK.

Don't confuse with: If it's growing somewhere damp and smells sweet there shouldn't be any confusion, but check out hemp agrimony as well.

Wildflowers of coasts

Low and tough plants that have to cope with salt and sea winds.

Thrift or sea pink (up to 25cm tall)

Identification: Forms cushions of very narrow leaves from which tall pompom pink flowers grow.

Fact: Can cope with dry salty ground, so you can find this growing on rocks, on sand dunes, or on grassland all around the coast.

Uses: Possibly because its growth is adapted to conserve water, it is associated with saving money, which maybe why it used to feature on the threepenny coin that was used in the UK until 1971.

Where to see it: Anywhere around the coast, but perhaps at its best in the western isles of Scotland.

Don't confuse with: Other pink coastal flowers, such as centaury and wild thyme. But they don't have the same combination of a cushion of leaves and tall flower stems.

Yellow horned poppy (up to 90cm tall)

Identification: Four bright yellow petals grow from pale, icy green clumps. The seed pods can be 30cm long and are very thin. They look a bit like horns, hence the name.

Fact: Only found naturally growing on coastal shingle beaches, where it can help to hold the beach together, but also grows on railway tracks.

Uses: Yellow horned poppy is poisonous to people, but may have medicinal uses.

Where to see it: It's quite sensitive to disturbance and trampling, so look for quieter parts of shingle beaches.

Don't confuse with: Field poppies, which have flowers of the same shape but they are red and grow in fields or evening primrose and mulleins, which both have yellow flowers but they grow from a flower spike, not from a rosette.

Wildflowers of grassland

Grasses grow from the base, so that animals nibbling from the top don't harm them. These flowers live among the grass.

Grasses

Grasses aren't just the plants between the wildflowers – they are wildflowers!

Meadow foxtail (up to 1m tall)

Identification: The flower heads do look like the tails of very tiny foxes.

Fact: Flowers early in the year and often causes the first flush of hay fever for sufferers.

Uses: Grown for animals to eat and to store as hay for winter food.

Where to see it: In farmland and along road verges throughout the UK.

Don't confuse with: There are two similar species of grass among our 200 or so similar grasses, rushes and sedges.

Common reed (up to 3m tall)

Identification: This is the plant that makes up reedbeds, an important habitat for wildlife. It grows in dense patches in wetlands, along riverbanks and can even cope with salt water in estuaries.

Fact: In the right conditions, common reed can spread up to three metres a year, so it can swamp an area if left undisturbed.

Uses: As well as being a great habitat for wildlife, common reeds are used for thatching roofs.

Where to see it: Along slow rivers and the edges of lakes, but at its best in nature reserves.

Don't confuse with: Planted crops of sweetcorn or wheat, because they grow so densely.

White clover (flowers 1.5-2cm across)

Identification: White pompom flowers that may have a pink tinge. Leaves have three lobes, but finding four-leaved versions is considered lucky.

Fact: Clovers have the ability to take nitrogen gas from the air and fix it in their roots whereas most plants have to take nitrogen from the soil. This means that clover can grow in poorer soil than many plants.

Uses: White clover is grown as a green manure, but is also prized by beekeepers because it produces lots of nectar for their bees to make honey from.

Where to see it: Most grasslands, including lawns, will have clover in them, but it may be mown before it flowers. Look for darker patches in the lawn and then spot the leaves.

Don't confuse with: Red clover, which is much taller and has red flowers.

Common spotted orchid (up to 40cm tall)

Identification: One tall flower spike per plant rising straight up from a rosette of oval-spotted leaves. Individual flowers can range from white via the more usual pale pink to purple.

Fact: Orchids produce some of the smallest seeds in the plant world, and depend on a fungus to help them grow – no fungus, no orchid.

Uses: This is one of the few wildflowers that looks so exotic that people grow it for the simple enjoyment of its appearance.

Where to see it: Throughout the UK, mainly on damp grassland and even into open woodland, but especially on chalky soils.

Don't confuse with: Heath spotted orchid, which has round spots on its leaves, or fragrant orchid (it smells lovely!) which has spotless leaves. There are over 50 kinds of orchid in the UK.

Wildflowers of heathland

These flowers have to live in very poor, often quite acidic soils.

Round-leaved sundew (rosette up to 5cm)

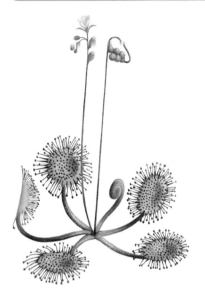

Identification: Round, crimson leaves, each dotted with glittering sticky droplets.

Fact: Sundews need insects to supplement their diets, but don't need them to pollinate their flowers – they can do that themselves.

Use: This plant is a fly killer! Its sticky leaves trap insects and then digest them to supplement its diet.

Where to see it: On bogs, fens and heathlands throughout the UK. Look around the edges of heathland ponds because sundews like wet feet.

Don't confuse with: The other species of sundews in the UK have different-shaped leaves, but all look quite similar.

Bell heather (up to 60cm tall)

Identification: Thin, needle-like leaves on a low bushy plant, but distinctive small bell or lantern-shaped pink flowers.

Fact: This flower lives on poor heathland soils, but is particularly found on the drier parts of the heath. It's not unusual to see it growing along the side of heathland paths because people choose the drier places to walk too.

Uses Bell heather plants were used to make animal bedding and brooms.

Where to see it: On dry heaths throughout the UK, but it is also grown in rockeries.

Don't confuse with: Ling, or common heather, which looks similarly bushy, but has tiny, open pink flowers with four petals.

Wildflowers of woodland

These usually flower early in the year, before the tree leaves block out the light.

Primrose (plant 10cm tall)

Identification: Rosette of slightly crinkly pale green leaves, with up to a dozen or so delicate pale yellow flowers growing one per stem from the centre.

Fact: Look closely at the flowers on different plants and you will see they come in two types, called pin and thrum. They have to mate with each other.

Uses: The flowers used to be made into a country wine and some people used to eat the leaves, but primroses aren't as common as they used to be, so leave them for everyone to enjoy.

Where to see it: In woodland and old hedgerows, flowering in early spring before the tree canopy comes into leaf.

Don't confuse with: The cowslip, which is a darker yellow and has several flowers on each stem.

Wood anemone (up to 30cm tall)

Identification: Six petals (but sometimes more) on a white flower. Leaves look rather ragged.

Fact: The flowers open in the sunshine and track the movement of the sun across the sky. In dull or wet weather, they remain closed with their heads down.

Uses: Although the plant is poisonous, it is often grown in parks and gardens as well as living truly wild.

Where to see it: In damp mixed or deciduous woodland or old hedgerows and country road verges throughout the UK.

Don't confuse with: The flowers are much bigger than the other white flowers that grow in similar places, such as greater stitchwort.

Wildflowers of waste ground

These flowers hardly need any soil to grow in – a crack in hard ground is enough.

Rosebay-willowherb or fireweed (up to 2m tall)

Identification: Tall, upright plant with small pink flowers. More often growing in drifts than on its own.

Fact: Colonises bare ground such as fire sites. Spread rapidly in the UK in the 18th century, following the development of the railway network, and again following the bombing of World War II.

Uses: Young leaves used to be eaten by Native Americans but more rarely in the UK.

Where to see it: Any bare or disturbed ground, such as railway tracks, abandoned building sites and new road cuttings.

Don't confuse with: Great and hoary willowherbs, which are both much hairier.

Buddleia (bush up to about 4m high)

Identification: A garden escapee so plenty of varieties. Most common has cone-like clusters of small purple or white flowers.

Fact: Pushes its way into cracks in concrete and pavements, especially in waste ground.

Uses: Widely planted as a garden plant to attract feeding butterflies, which most varieties do well, but it's useless for most caterpillars.

Where to see it: Almost anywhere in towns and cities, even growing out of old walls and chimneys!

Don't confuse with: Other bushy garden escapes such as lilac.

Lower plants

Not lower to the ground, just more primitive. They don't flower but are just as interesting. They include mosses, ferns and seaweeds.

Hart's-tongue fern (leaves up to 60cm long)

Identification: A wavy rosette of bright green leaves all year round, with scribbly brown markings underneath.

Behaviour: Grows in dark damp places, such as on canal lock gates, wet country lanes, river banks and dark woodland.

Uses: It used to be made into a medicine to treat all sorts of ailments, but it may not have worked at all.

Where to see it: Grows throughout the UK, but is less common in the far north.

Don't confuse with: There are over 60 different wild ferns in the UK, but the hart's tongue is distinctive.

Sphagnum bog moss (leaves a few mm long)

Identification: Sphagnum can be red, yellow, brown or green. It grows in great multi-coloured carpets as the main plant of many of our uplands.

Behaviour: Sphagnum is the main bog plant and holds a huge amount of water.

Uses: Sphagnum rots down to form peat, which is used as a fuel or for planting garden flowers. It is much better left in the wild, though.

Where to see it: Bogs and uplands across the UK are covered in sphagnums.

Don't confuse with: There are at least 10 similar sphagnum species in the UK and perhaps 300 worldwide.

Bladder wrack (up to 40cm long)

Identification: A strong central rib and round, marble-sized bladders make this green or black seaweed stand out.

Fact: Clings to stones along sheltered coasts. Its bladders help it to float in the water to get as much light as possible.

Uses: This was the original source of iodine that was used to treat people with thyroid problems.

Where to see it: Mainly on sheltered North Sea coasts, but you can find it on the tideline anywhere.

Don't confuse with: Rockweed, which has slimmer fronds and egg-shaped bladders.

Sea belt (up to 3m long)

Identification: Broad but crinkly-looking brown seaweed, sometimes washed up after a storm.

Fact: Grows from just below low tide to around 30m deep and sometimes attaches itself to big rocks rather than the seabed.

Uses: Was a source of sweetener during World War II.

Where to see it: Washed up on a beach anywhere around our coasts.

Don't confuse with: The other big seaweeds, such as oarweed, which don't have the wavy form.

Fungi

Are they animals? Certainly not. Are they plants? Hmm, much trickier. Many people think fungi are plants because they mostly grow from the ground and don't move around much. But really they are separate, neither animal nor plant, a group of their own.

The fungi we see are usually just like the fruits on an apple tree. The main fungus itself remains hidden within the soil or growing through the rotting wood of a tree. It's there all year, but we mostly see fungi in the autumn, especially after rain, when most of them pop up very quickly as mushrooms or toadstools. Others, such as the bracket fungi or the blobby King Alfred's cakes, can be seen all year round.

Be careful

Some fungi are great to eat, others would make you sick, and taking even a small bite from some would see you die a horrible, painful death. Some of the really nasty ones look and even smell very much like the edible ones. It's safer not to eat any wild fungi at all. And remember to wash your hands after touching any fungi.

Identifying fungi can be really difficult, but a few things to look for are the overall shape and colour, how the underside of the cap of the toadstools looks, and the colour of the spores. Spores are like a fungus's seeds. Take a fresh toadstool cap, put it on white paper and leave it overnight, covered with a bowl. In the morning, some of the spores will have dropped onto the paper in an interesting pattern. You can preserve this with a little bit of hairspray.

Remember to wash your hands after touching any fungi, like this shaggy ink cap.

Mushrooms and toadstools are nature's great recyclers, breaking dead things down for regrowth.

Fly agaric (up to 30cm across)

Identification: The classic fairytale toadstool, usually with white spots on the red cap. White stem with a frill near the top.

Uses: In olden days, it was used to kill insects in milk.

Fact: This toadstool is poisonous but very rarely kills people because it is so easy to identify – unless its white spots have rubbed off in the rain!

Where to see it: In woodlands or old grasslands across the UK. It lives on both pine and broad-leaved tree roots.

Don't confuse with: There are many other red toadstools and other more dangerous species in the same family but they have pale caps.

Giant puffball (up to 70cm across)

Identification: A huge pale ball of a fungus that may be either out in the open in a meadow or hidden in a woodland.

Uses: Fresh giant puffballs can be eaten, but they often get used as footballs!

Fact: If all the spores in a single giant puffball grew up, they would weigh more than the whole world – clearly they don't!

Where to see it: Never common, but in meadows, hedgerows and woodlands throughout the UK from late summer.

Don't confuse with: Very young ones may look like smaller fungi, but fully grown they may look like a football!

Sulphur tuft (up to 6cm across)

Identification: Bright yellow fungus, usually more orange in the centre and paler around the edge. Grows in bunches, often the only fungus around.

Uses: Foresters may be able to use sulphur-tuft to help wipe out a fungal disease of pine trees.

Fact: Like many of our fungi, sulphur tuft is bitter-tasting and poisonous.

Where to see it: Grows from rotting wood, usually near the ground. Common on old logs or rotting tree stumps throughout the UK.

Don't confuse with: There are over 15,000 species of fungi in the UK, but the one most similar to this is conifer tuft, which is browner and lives only in pinewoods.

Birch bracket (up to 30cm across)

Identification: Pale brown on top and white and spongy looking underneath, rather than frilly like the other fungi in this book.

Uses: The final sharpening polish or 'strop' on old-style razors used to be made with this fungus, which is sometimes called 'razor-strop'.

Fact: It always grows with the spongy underside facing downwards, so if you find one on the ground on a branch, you can work out which angle it grew at.

Where to see it: On old, sickly and dead birch trees throughout the UK.

Don't confuse with: There are many other bracket fungi, but this is the most common, so long as you are looking at the right sort of tree.

Fly agaric can be found in woodlands or old grasslands across the UK.

Wildlife Activities

Make a weather vane

April showers again, and you're stuck indoors. Wouldn't life be easier with your own weather forecast? Well you can start by making a weather vane.

A weather vane measures wind direction. The wind makes it spin around and point in the direction the wind is coming from. This tells you what the wind might be like. For example, a south wind is usually warm (because it comes from the south), while a north wind is usually cold (because ... you guessed it!)

Pointing at the wind

All weather vanes have an arrow-shaped end, which turns into the wind, and a wider end, which catches the breeze and makes it turn.

You will need

Cardboard
(an old cardboard box will do)

Pen

Scissors

Tape

Thin stick (a wooden skewer/
kebab stick is perfect)

Drinking straw

Hammer and nail

Plastic soft drink
bottle with cap

Sand

Compass

Here's how you can make your own, using just cardboard.

❶ Mark out a large arrow on the cardboard to the shape and measurements shown below. Then cut it out..

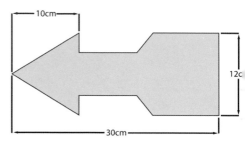

❷ Tape one end of the wooden skewer to the arrow and insert the other end in the straw. The skewer should turn freely inside the straw.

❸ Make a hole in the bottle cap (a grown-up will help), just large enough to hold the straw firmly. Then push the straw through. Fill the bottom of the bottle with sand.

❹ Fit the straw into the bottle and do up the cap. The straw should be upright, the arrow should turn freely and the bottle should remain steady.

5 Use a compass or a map to work out where north is (maps always have north at the top of the page). Then mark the directions of north, south, east and west on the bottle – or on the surface where you place it.

NORTH

Set it up

Place your weather vane somewhere it will catch the breeze – on top of a wall is good – and watch what happens. Remember, the arrow always points in the direction that the wind is coming from. Bring it in when it rains.

Customise!

Weather vanes work in many different shapes and materials. You could make one out of wood, if you're good at woodwork, or decorate it with a cockerel – like the ones you see on church roofs. The important things are that the arrow turns freely, you know where north is, and that it doesn't blow away.

LOG IT Weather report

USE YOUR NATURE DIARY

Try checking your weather vane twice a day, and keep this up for a week. Note down the wind direction and any other weather you notice, too – such as whether it is sunny or raining.

Day	Time	Wind	Weather
Monday			
Tuesday			
Wednesday			
Thursday			
Friday			

Baths for birds

Water is just as important as food. Garden birds need to drink regularly and keep their feathers clean. You can help them out with a birdbath.

Keep it shallow

There are many different ways to make a birdbath. A good one should not be too deep, and should have gently sloping sides so that any other creatures that tumble in can easily get out. Fill it with no more than 8 cm (3 in) of water. Here are two ideas:

Clay plant-pot saucer Set the saucer down on the ground or on top of an upturned clay pot.

Hanging pie dish If you don't have enough garden space for a birdbath on the ground, you could set a ceramic, deep-dish, pie plate inside a hanging basket and hang it from a branch. Some water will splash out so remember to refil it regularly.

Buy a birdbath You don't have to make a birdbath. You can buy all kinds of birdbaths, including some fancy, expensive ones. But birds won't care how much you spend, just so long as you give them clean, regular water.

Birdbath tips

- Put in small rocks, or something else for birds to perch on.

- The bottom needs a fairly rough surface to give the birds a solid footing. You could add gravel.

- Place it somewhere out of reach of pouncing cats, but not too exposed. Birds often perch on nearby branches to scan for danger before they come to drink.

- Raise it above ground to keep it safer from cats.

- Clean it every couple of weeks using hot water, to keep the water clear and prevent disease spreading. Remember to wash your hands afterwards.

- Top it up more often during summer – water evaporates quickly in hot weather.

- In winter, keep it free of ice. Cold water thaws ice more quickly than hot water. (A floating tennis ball can also stop ice forming.)

LOG IT

DIARY USE YOUR NATURE

Who wants a drink?

Use the table below to record which birds visit your birdbath.
One example is included to start you off.

Species	Date	How many?
Blackbird	1 Dec	1

A GOOD GULP

FOCUS

Watch how pigeons drinking at your birdbath spend longer with their heads down. They are the only British birds that can drink by sucking water up. Other birds have to take a sip then raise their heads to let the water trickle down their throat. Pigeons eat mostly dry grain and seeds, so they need a lot of water.

Make a nestbox

Do you have blue tits in your garden? Then why not put up a nest box for them? Better get cracking, so it's ready for the breeding season in early spring.

Boxing clever

Blue tits need a nest box with a small hole, just like the tree holes they use in the wild. You can buy one from the RSPB or other good suppliers. But it's cheaper to make your own – and more fun, too. Here's how:

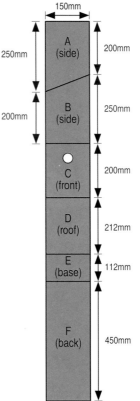

You will need

One plank of wood: 150 cm (60 in) long, 15 cm (6 in) wide, and 1.5 cm (0.6 in) thick.

Pencil and ruler

25 nails (galvanised nails last longer) or woodscrews

Hammer – or a screwdriver if you're using woodscrews

Wire

Saw

A brace and bit

A piece of thick rubber, approx. 15 cm (6 in) by 10 cm (4 in) (from the inner tube of a bicycle tyre, for example)

A grown-up – to help with the tricky bits

❶ Use the ruler and pencil to mark out the plank of wood. Follow the above diagram exactly.

Ask a grown-up to saw the plank into six separate parts along the lines marked in the diagram.

sk a grown-up to cut out the hole in piece C (the front) using the brace and bit. The hole should be 2.5 cm (1 in) wide and at least 12 cm (5 in) from the bottom.

❶ Nail or screw the pieces together following the diagram – all except for piece D (the roof). Again, a grown-up can help.

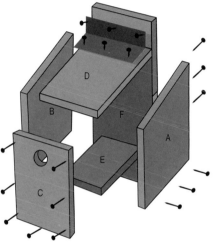

The hole truth

Other birds use bigger holes: great tits need them 2.8 cm wide; house sparrows and nuthatches need 3.2 cm (1.3 in) wide. Some birds, such as robins, prefer open-fronted boxes.

❶ Use the piece of rubber as the hinge for the roof: nail one side to the roof and the other side to the back of the box.

❶ Put in one screw on the roof and another on the side of the box near the top. Then make a catch from a piece of wire to keep the roof closed.

❶ Fix your nest box at least 2 metres (6.5 feet) high on a tree or wall, facing somewhere between north and east to protect it from bad weather. Do it before mid-February so it is ready for the start of the breeding season.

Nest box calendar

Looking after a nest box is a year-round job.

Spring If birds move in, leave them alone. Don't peep inside while the box is in use, but look out for youngsters making their first appearance.

Autumn Clean out the nest box when breeding is over (September onwards). Remove the nest and use boiling water to kill any bugs and germs.

Winter Once the box is clean and dry, add a small amount of clean hay or wood shavings. This may encourage mammals to hibernate in it – or birds to roost.

Plaster prints

Wild animals can be hard to spot. But their tracks tell you when they've been around. Here's a great way to keep a record of who trod where.

Track them down

Look for tracks beside water, around muddy fields or on damp sand. Go on a dry day, soon after it has rained. And set out early, before the tracks are spoiled.

You will need

Container of Plaster of Paris

Plastic bottle of water
(sea water is fine on the beach)

Cardboard strips, about 8 cm
(3 in) wide by 30 cm (12 in)
long

Plastic mixing bowl

Plastic mixing spoon

Newspaper

creamy, like pancake batter. Stir until all the lumps are gone. Be sure you mix enough to do the job.

❹ Gently spoon the plaster into the track. Make sure you fill in all details. Do not let it overflow the cardboard.

What to do

❶ Find a clear animal track and carefully remove any loose leaves or sticks.

❷ Make a low wall around the track with the cardboard strip. Tape the ends together and press it gently into the soil so no plaster will run away.

❸ Use a spoon to mix two parts Plaster of Paris with one part water in the mixing bowl. It should become thick and

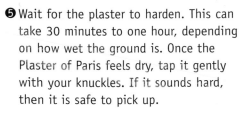

❺ Wait for the plaster to harden. This can take 30 minutes to one hour, depending on how wet the ground is. Once the Plaster of Paris feels dry, tap it gently with your knuckles. If it sounds hard, then it is safe to pick up.

❻ Lift the cast straight up. You may need to dig out some of the soil from underneath first, but do not pry with a stick. Carefully dust off any dirt and remove the cardboard ring.

❼ Pack your cast carefully in newspaper and take it home.

❽ Allow it to dry for several days before cleaning it or painting it.

Care for your casts

🐾 Never wrap plaster casts in plastic bags – this prevents moisture getting out. Clean your cast by holding it under
🐾 running water and gently rubbing away excess dirt.
🐾 Out-of-date Plaster of Paris may not set properly.
🐾 Never leave your cast soaking in water: it will start to soften.
🐾 If you paint your cast, leave one surface unpainted so moisture can escape.

More signs
Look out for other signs animals leave behind:
Hair on the bottom of a fence where a badger has wriggled underneath
Hazelnut shells: split in two means a squirrel; neat hole means a mouse or vole
Pine cones stripped by a squirrel

Who is it?
Can you identify what animal made the print in your cast? Look to see whether it has hooves, like a deer, or pads and toes, like a fox. Look for claw marks (cat tracks don't show claws) and count the toes. A book on tracks will help. Here are some you might find.

Fox Like a dog, but longer and thinner.

Badger Five toes and long claws.

Rabbit Back foot (right) bigger than front foot (left).

Squirrel Small, with tiny fingers.

Roe deer A neat shield split in half.

Draw a badger

Badgers' stripy faces make them easy to identify. But they're not so easy to draw. That's partly because their real shape is hidden under all that fur.

Quick on the draw!

Here's how to draw a badger in five easy steps. You will need paper and a pencil. And coloured pencils, if you want to colour it in.

Step 1 ▶

Draw a longish oval for the body and, above it to the left, a smaller pear shape for the head. Tilt the pear upwards slightly – this will make the badger look livelier. Leave plenty of space for the neck: badgers have long necks under all that fur.

Step 2 ▶

Draw two smooth lines to link the head to the body. Use four more simple lines to show where the legs will go – these are a little longer than you may think.

Step 3 ▶

Draw around the body shape again and add the fur. The body fur comes halfway down the legs. Now complete the legs. The back feet are longer than the front feet and you can see claws on all the feet.

Step 4 ▶

Give your badger a face by adding an eye, nose and ears. Place the eye halfway between the nose and ear. A white dot near the top of the black eye will make it look shiny and alive. A small line will work for the nose. Don't worry about the mouth – you can't really see it at this angle.

Step 5 ▶

Draw two thick black stripes – one starting from just in front of each eye, and passing back through the eye and ear to join the dark body fur. The rest of the head is white, and the white fur extends a little way down the back and along the sides of the neck. Colour the body greyish-brown, with black legs and throat. Fine downward lines help show the furry coat. The tips of the ears are white.

Softly, softly

- ◗ Draw softly in pencil for steps 1–4. That way, once you're happy with the shape, you can rub out any lines you don't need.

- ◗ Get the shape right first; the colours and markings can follow later.

- ◗ Between each step, take a look at your drawing from across the room. Does the shape look right? If not, tweak it until you're happy. Always get the shape right first; the details can follow.

Big stoat   FOCUS

Badgers belong to the same family as stoats and weasels. They have a similar shape, with a long body and short legs, which is great for squeezing down holes. Badgers look fatter because of their thick fur, but really they are quite slim.

Hedgehog house

Do hedgehogs ever visit your garden? Perhaps they come at night, in secret. You can encourage them in by giving them a safe winter home.

Make it cosy

As autumn nights draw in, hedgehogs are looking for a safe, snug place in which to spend the winter. They collect leaves, grass, straw, bracken and other dry vegetation to build their own nests. For your hedgehog house you need to make something that looks and feels just like this.

❶ Choose a suitable site for your hedgehog home. It should be a quiet undisturbed spot, up against a bank, fence or hedge.

❷ Cut small air slits on each side of the box, and an entrance about 15 cm (6 in) wide in the front.

❸ Place the box in position upside down.

❹ Put some shredded newspapers and clean dry grass inside (but not too much, as hedgehogs prefer to gather their own bedding).

❺ Cover the top of the box with the plastic sheeting.

You will need
An old, sturdy cardboard box
A small piece of plastic sheeting
(e.g. an old plastic bag)
Stones, earth, dry grass, twigs and leaves
Dry grass and/or shredded paper
Scissors

❻ Pile twigs around and over the box to make a small dome, then cover this with dry grass, stones, earth and leaves until the box is hidden.

❼ Now leave it alone. With luck, you'll attract a prickly visitor to spend winter in your garden. If it's a female, she may even have her babies there in spring.

DID YOU KNOW? A hedgehog is pale pink at birth with its spines still beneath the skin. Within hours the spines begin to grow through. DID YOU KNOW? DID YOU KNOW? DID YOU KNOW?

TOP TIP

For a ready-made hedgehog home you can use an old, upturned crate. Ask a grown-up to help you remove the inside partitions and cut an entrance.

HIBERNATION FOCUS

Hedgehogs get their energy from food such as slugs and insects. But during winter this becomes harder to find. So they save energy by going into a kind of deep sleep, called hibernation. Their body temperature drops and their heartbeat and breathing slow down.

Helpful hedgehog hints

- To avoid cold winter winds make sure the entrance does not face north or north-east. A south-facing entrance is best.

- Leave a supply of grass and twigs outside the entrance: the hedgehog may take this in as extra bedding.

- Clean the box out in spring. But first make sure there is no hedgehog still inside it.

- Always check compost heaps and piles of firewood before disturbing them, as hedgehogs may nest there.

Draw an oak tree

Drawing a tree is easy, right? Just a big lollipop of leaves stuck on a long brown stick. But drawing a *good* one is trickier. Here's how to do it properly.

Branch lines

The secret to drawing a tree is understanding its shape. That's why winter is a good time to start, when the leaves have fallen and you can see how the branches are arranged underneath. You will need paper and a pencil – and coloured pencils if you want to colour it in.

Step 1 ▶

Start with the outline of the whole tree. Draw a large circle with a flattish base that almost fills the page. Remember, an oak tree is as wide as it is tall. Then add the bottom part of the trunk. It is shorter than you might think.

◀ Step 2

Draw the main branches of the tree. They start to fork and divide low down (right at the base of your outline circle). Don't make them too even or symmetrical; each one should go off at its own crazy angles – and some twist behind others.

Step 3 ▶

Now add the thinner side branches. Take them right up to the edge of the outline circle. Each branch divides into other branches, each of which divides in turn. The branches get thinner as you move out towards the edges.

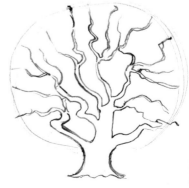

Step 4 ▶

Finally add the twigs at the ends of the branches. These are too small to see individually, so just shade with the side of your pencil to give the impression of lots of little twigs. If you're using colour, shade the trunk and branches.

You could turn your winter tree into a summer tree by adding leaves. Just cut out a piece of green paper to fit exactly over your original outline. Give it a nice clumpy edge and cut a few holes so you can see through. Use Magic Tape to stick it down, so you can remove it and show the branches underneath.

Shaping up

No two trees look the same. Every species has its own distinctive shape, and each individual tree differs from the next, depending upon what kind of soil it grows in and how much light it gets. An oak tree in dense woodland grows taller and thinner than one in the middle of a field.

Here are the shapes of three common trees: beech, silver birch and hazel. Can you tell which is which? Answers at the bottom.

DID YOU KNOW? There are more than 400 different kinds of oak tree worldwide.

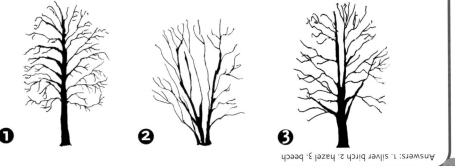

❶   ❷   ❸

Answers: 1. silver birch 2. hazel 3. beech

Glossary

Albino: white or partly white plumage that is not usually white.

Arable field: a field in which crops are grown.

Auk: a type of diving seabird, such as guillemot or puffin.

Bib: a patch of colour on a bird or animal's chin and throat, shaped like a baby's bib.

Bird recorder: a person who keeps official records of birds.

Bivalve: a shellfish with two shells, usually of the same shape.

Bracket fungus: a fungus that grows from the side of a rotting tree or old stump, often looking a bit like a shelf.

Breeding plumage: a bird's plumage while breeding and preparing to breed (usually early spring to summer).

Broad-leaved tree: one with wider leaves than pine needles. Most drop them for the winter (except holly).

Brood: young birds hatched from a single clutch of eggs.

Canopy: the top part of a tree or forest, with dense leaves and branches.

Carnivorous: meat-eating, and often without eating much else.

Chestnut: reddish-brown, like the colour of horse chestnut (conker).

Clearfell: an area in a woodland where all the trees have just been removed.

Clutch: group of eggs laid together in the same nest.

Cold-blooded: all creatures except birds and mammals need to use the sun's heat to warm up so they can move around. This is known as being cold-blooded.

Colony: a group of creatures breeding close together.

Cover: an area where you can't easily be seen, such as behind a bush.

Crepuscular: active at dawn and dusk.

Crofting: farming life on some Scottish islands.

Crown: the top part of a bird's head.

Dawn chorus: many birds singing together at the start of a spring day.

Deciduous: of trees, having leaves that all fall off together in the autumn.

Display flight: a special flight that some male birds use to attract females.

Diurnal: active during the day.

Diving duck: a species of duck, such as the Tufted Duck, that feeds mostly by diving under water.

Dorsal fin: the fin on the back of a fish, dolphin or whale. You won't see one on a seal.

Drumming: the mechanical courtship noise made by a woodpecker banging on a tree or a snipe vibrating its tail feathers in flight.

Dune slack: the marshy area behind some sand dunes.

Eclipse plumage: a male duck's plumage during moult, when it looks like a female.

Eyepieces: the parts of a telescope or pair of binoculars that you look through

Feeding party: a mixed group of small birds that get together outside the breeding season to find food.

Feral: descended from a domesticated species, but living wild.

Field guide: a book that helps you to identify wildlife.

Fieldmark: a special feature of a bird's plumage that helps you to identify it.

Fledgling: a young bird that gets its first adult feathers, ready for flying.

Flush: to cause a bird to fly off by walking too close to it.

Forage: search for food on the ground or among vegetation.

Forewing: the front part of a bird's wing in flight.

Game bird: a type of plump ground bird, such as pheasant or red grouse.

Gravel pit: a hole dug to collect gravel for building, that has been flooded like a lake.

Habitat: the type of place in which a creature lives, such as woodland, an estuary or a rockpool.

Heathland: a southern lowland habitat, with sandy soil, heather, gorse and bogs.

Hide: somewhere from which to watch wildlife, where you can see out, while being hidden from creatures.

High tide line: the highest point that waves reach on a beach, often marked by seaweed.

Host bird: a bird, such as dunnock, in whose nests cuckoos lay their eggs.

Hover: the flying equivalent of running on the spot.

Hybrid: an animal or plant whose parents are two different species. Most animal hybrids can't breed themselves.

Identification: working out the name of a creature; sometimes known as ID.

Insect: a six-legged creature with a three-part body plan. Includes butterflies, ants and beetles, but not spiders.

Insectivorous: of a plant, one that catches and eats insects to help it grow.

Invertebrate: a creature without a backbone. Also known as a minibeast.

Jizz: the unique character of each bird species that you learn with experience.

Juvenile: not yet adult.

Key: a way of finding something out by answering simple questions.

Landscape: what somewhere looks like from a distance.

Lens tissue/cloth: a special cloth for wiping the lenses (glass parts) of binoculars, cameras or telescopes.

Local patch: an area near where you live, where you watch birds or animals regularly.

Maggot: the wriggling young grubs of flies or beetles, like dull caterpillars.

Glossary

Migrant: a creature that travels when the seasons change to find food and/or nest sites.

Migration: the regular seasonal movement of animals from one part of the world to another. Many birds and insects migrate hundreds or thousands of kilometres every year.

Minibeast: another word for invertebrate; any small creatures – insect, spider, slug, etc. Does not include any vertebrates, however small.

Mob: when birds chase off an unwelcome bird, such as a hawk, owl or cuckoo.

Moors/moorland: an open, upland habitat with heather, rocky and boggy ground, and very few trees.

Mudflats: wide areas of mud along the coast, exposed when the tide goes out.

Native: an animal or plant that has either always lived here or arrived under its own power is said to be native.

Necklace: a pattern around a bird's throat in the shape of a necklace.

Nestlings: baby birds, before they have left the nest.

Nocturnal: active at night.

Overwinter: to stay for the winter.

Passage migrant/visitor: a bird that passes through without stopping to breed or spend the winter.

Plantation: a forest of trees, such as pine trees, planted by people.

Plumage: the feathers of a bird seen as a whole. Summer and winter plumages may look very different for some birds.

Poisonous: has harmful or possibly deadly effects when eaten or touched. Some fungi and berries are poisonous, but very little UK wildlife is dangerous.

Predator: an animal or bird that hunts other animals for food.

Preen gland: a place on a bird's back that produces oil to keep its feathers clean.

Raptor: a bird of prey, such as a hawk, falcon or buzzard.

Reedbed: large area of reeds – usually beside water.

Reservoir: an artificial lake that people build to collect water.

Resident: living in one place all year.

Rhizomes: fat, root-like parts of a plants such as reed or irises that grow underground before sprouting up as new plants.

Roost: a place where birds spend the night – often in a group.

Scan: to try to spot something by looking over a wide area.

Scrub: low, dense vegetation such as bushes or small trees.

Seawatching: looking for birds on or over the sea.

Sett: a badger family's underground home.

Sheen: a shiny patch of colour on a bird's plumage that changes with the light.

Shingle: small stones on a beach.

Sociable: living mostly in groups.

Species: a group of similar animals or plants that live in the same area and can breed together enough to have grandchildren are of one species. House sparrows are a species, as are daisies and human beings.

Stalk: to creep up close to something without being seen.

Stubble field: a field with cut stalks, left after the crop has been harvested.

'T-bar': T-shaped marking at the end of a bird's tail (such as a wheatear's).

Tentacle: slim flexible tube or arm used for feeding, feeling or moving around. Usually found on invertebrates.

Toadstool: a fungus that looks like a mushroom, with a cap and stem.

Tracks: footprints or an animal pathway.

Ultraviolet light: light that we can't see, but that some animals can, such as moths or blue tits.

Underparts: the lower half of a bird, including its throat, breast, belly and vent.

Undulating: the up-and-down pattern of some birds' flight, including woodpeckers.

Uplands: high-altitude areas, such as hills, moorland and mountains.

Upperparts: the upper half of a bird, including its head, neck, back, folded wings and rump.

'V' formation: a shape like the letter V, made by a flock of flying birds, such as geese.

Vegetarian: an animal (or person) that eats only or mainly plants.

Vertebrate: an animal with a backbone: mammals, birds, reptiles, amphibians and fishes, but nothing else.

Wader: birds with long legs and (usually) long bills that mostly feed in shallow water or along the shore, such as curlews, sandpipers and plovers.

Warm-blooded: being able to work whatever the outside temperature. Birds and mammals are warm-blooded.

Wattle: bright, fleshy skin on a bird's face.

Wetland: a habitat dominated by water, such as a lake or marsh.

Wildfowl: any species of duck, goose or swan.

Species Index

Species Index

RSPB Wildlife Explorers

If you've enjoyed this book, then you'll love RSPB Wildlife Explorers. It's the biggest wildlife club for children in the world!

You'll get some great stuff when you join. For starters, you'll receive your very own membership pack bursting with goodies, plus six magazines a year, each of them packed with fascinating facts, games, competitions and things to do. You'll discover more about amazing wildlife – from skydiving peregrines to hibernating hedgehogs – and learn what to look out for throughout the year, so that you can put your newfound wildlife watching skills into practice.

And becoming a member also means that you'll be helping the RSPB look after nature here in the UK, and around the world. That's everything from puffins nesting on British cliffs to tigers in the rainforests of Sumatra. So what are you waiting for? Join today and discover a world of wildlife. **Find out more at www.rspb.org.uk/join**